Receiving the Council

D1416761

Receiving the Council

Theological and Canonical Insights and Debates

Ladislas Orsy

A Michael Glazier Book

LITURGICAL PRESS
Collegeville, Minnesota

www.litpress.org

A Michael Glazier Book published by Liturgical Press

Cover design by David Manahan, OSB. Photo © Ackab and Dreamstime.com

Joseph Cardinal Ratzinger, "Stellungnahme," in *Stimmen der Zeit* 217 (1999) 169–72 and "Schlusswort zur Debatte mit Pater Orsy," in *Stimmen der Zeit* 217 (1999) 420–22. © Libreria Editrice Vaticana. Reprinted with permission.

1   2   3   4   5   6   7   8   9

Library of Congress Cataloging-in-Publication Data

Orsy, Ladislas M., 1921–
    Receiving the Council : theological and canonical insights and debates / Ladislas Orsy.
      p. cm.
    "A Michael Glazier book."
    Includes bibliographical references and index.
    ISBN 978-0-8146-5377-7
    1. Vatican Council (2nd : 1962–1965).   2. Catholic Church—History—20th century.   3. Church renewal—Catholic Church.   I. Title.
BX8301962 .O89   2009
262'.52—dc22
                                                     2009028706

To the memory of

ANGELO GIOVANNI RONCALLI
BLESSED JOHN XXIII

Era un papa che ti ha fatto sentire come una persona
"He was a pope who made you feel like a person"

(Remark by an anonymous ticket collector on a Roman bus,
the morning after *Papa Giovanni* left his people,
June 4, 1963.)

If Christianity be an universal religion, suited not simply to one locality or period but to all times and places, it cannot but vary in its relations and dealings towards the world around it, that is, it will develop.

Principles require a very various application according as persons and circumstances vary, and must be thrown into new shapes according to the form of society which they are to influence.

John Henry Newman
An Essay on the Development of Christian Doctrine
Chapter II, Section I, 3

Contents

Acknowledgments

To whom am I indebted? I keep asking myself, and my memory responds by recalling good and learned persons who contributed to the development of my mind. To list them all would be fair but not feasible; to name a few is a matter of duty.

In the past, at privileged times, I met teachers or friends (not with us anymore) who opened up new fields of vision for me and changed the direction of my thinking. The impact of such meetings never wore off. In the beginning of my academic studies, Alois Naber, S.J., from Germany, then professor of history of philosophy at the Gregorian University, Rome, introduced me to the fascinating story of Western philosophy from antiquity to modernity; his gentle and good-humored lectures are still guiding me on a field that otherwise I may have found a labyrinth with no exit. In my first encounter with theology, Leopold Malevez, S.J., professor of theology at Collège St. Albert de Louvain, Belgium, warned me against ever having a "hero" among theologians and taught me how to approach the mysteries independently and how to reach critically sound judgments using authentic sources—without following favored opinions. The admonition took: I never joined a school. When I was in Rome again, for the study of canon law, Peter Huizing, S.J., a native of the Netherlands, professor at the Gregorian University and an insightful historian, drew my attention to the fragility of human institutions even in the community of believers, and to the ever-present temptation to revere the transient as if it were permanent. Further, I am indebted to Barry Nicholas, Esq., fellow and later Master of Brasenose College, Oxford, England; with his finely tuned expertise in comparative legal studies, he helped me to master the intricacies of common law and to give due attention to the empirical realities in the realm of law.

Once I began teaching at the Gregorian University in Rome, I increasingly sensed the need to understand better "what it means to understand" and to find a method that could bring fresh water to parched minds—this happened in the vibrant years of the *aggiornamento.* I found in-house help: Bernard

Lonergan, S.J., was professor of theology and an elder colleague of mine at the same institution. We conversed, and I studied his *Insight.* The result: I progressed in the art of raising well-grounded and correctly directed questions, reached some new insights in my own field, and became more cautious in asserting "the truth." A lifelong gift.

Now, from the past to the present.

For many years Georgetown University Law Center, whose motto is "Law is but the means—justice is the end," has given me an intellectual home: it is an "academy" of abundant insights and vigorous debates. Professor Judy Areen, Esq., former dean, invited me to join the school. Dean Alexander Aleinikoff, Esq., continued to support my work. Carol O'Neil, Esq., associate dean, took every opportunity to encourage my efforts.

The Jesuit community at Georgetown University provided for all my needs: may my gratitude match their generosity. In particular Ronald Murphy, S.J., has been my literary counselor for years; he knows how to read beyond the lines and communicate wisdom with style.

Throughout all my teaching years, curious students kept my mind alert with their questions. But how to thank such benefactors who come and go? I hereby propose that in the quadrangle of every university a monument should be erected dedicated to the "Anonymous Inquiring Students" who keep the teachers' minds fresh. Waiting for that, let this paragraph do the honors.

In the preparation of the manuscript many pairs of eyes and hands helped me: Megan Hall, Esq., and Joshua Kellemen, my research assistants, worked long days and weeks in editing the chapters. Sharon Doku, Esq., as research assistant, and Dr. Josie Ryan, as volunteer, shared the intense labor of the last revisions.

From Liturgical Press, Hans Christoffersen watched over the progress of my work and made sure of its timely completion. Mary Stommes provided good advice for style and content. Dr. Linda Maloney rendered into English sensitive German documents.

To all generous givers, named or not, my heartfelt thanks.

Prologue

Every time Christians gather and make their profession of faith, reciting the *symbolum* composed by the councils of Nicea (325) and Constantinople (381), they implicitly proclaim their faith in the power of the ecumenical councils. After all, two of those councils composed the well-known Creed.

Such gatherings of the bishops are mysterious events in the history of God's dealing with his people. The councils appear fully human, but, ever since their beginnings in 325 in Nicea, the communities perceive them as authentic witnesses of faith—assisted by the Spirit of Christ and endowed with a gift of fidelity to the evangelical message.

Vatican Council II, which opened on October 11, 1962, was no less an ecumenical council than any other held in the first or second millennium (twenty of them)—no matter how different it may have been in its style and orientation. It had its human moments in conflicts and compromises, but ultimately it was an intensely creative period in faith seeking (and finding!) understanding—*fides quaerens intellectum.*

The day of its closing, December 8, 1965, was both a conclusion and a beginning. The bishops went home; their special task ended. Now the people must continue the search for understanding, reach new insights, proclaim the message in a fresh way so as to bring light to the nations and to bring hope to those who are sitting in the shadow of death.

In this venture, the people are no less assisted by the Spirit than was the Council. Of course, the human struggles continue: dissonant voices are heard and fierce fights are fought—just as it happened among the bishops assembled. But ultimately the Spirit of God "hovers over this world" and does not—will not—fail to assist God's servants.

Our times are the times for the reception of the Council. No less is asked from us, both individuals and communities, than to enter into the dynamics of the Council and to undergo a conversion to a new vision and new practices.

My intent for this book is to speak about this fresh vision and then to point to new and needed practices that correspond to the vision. Reflective as my chapters may be, experience played its part in their conception. I had the opportunity to witness the event of the Council and to follow its development from its convocation to its end. I lectured at the Gregorian University from 1960 through 1966, teaching topics passionately debated at the Council: episcopal collegiality, law and conscience, and so forth. I served as regular expert for an archbishop (hence, was in possession of circulating schemata, drafts, and scripts of debates) and conversed with members of the venerable body over pasta and *vino dei castelli*.

The literary form pursued in this book is of overriding importance for the interpretation of what it contains. I wish to present my opinions as insights proposed for debate. Nothing more, nothing less. Now, insights are precious, but they are also fragile. They are precious because they are attempts to go beyond the obvious—they are fruits of a creative process, a flash of light in the dark. They are fragile because, as yet, they have not been confirmed by a critical scrutiny. They do not represent the truth; they are attempts to reach the truth.

In probing the insights, a good step forward is to offer them to the living community: let the believers' sense of faith judge them. Let the insights become disputed questions.

Disputations in the spirit of openness and charity always had a place of pride in the intellectual history of the Christian community. St. Thomas of Aquinas was a supreme master of it. He liked to preface his affirmations by contrasting questions.

Such a venerable tradition should not become extinct. After all, the entire body of the faithful has been entrusted with the fullness of the evangelical message. Hence, no one should ever be left out of the process of seeking its fuller understanding.

In the spirit of this heritage, I include in the book a disputation in its integrity (chapter 9). It is of some significance; in it (then) Cardinal Joseph Ratzinger (later Pope Benedict XVI) responds *as a theologian* to an article of mine on the issue of definitive teaching. There, the future pope reveals his mind concerning a major issue with far-reaching consequences. He gives, also, interesting details about the composition and publication of the relevant documents of the Holy See.

Further, he showed his active interest in the question of the theological nature and canonical structure of the episcopal conferences, although without personally entering into a debate (see chapter 2, Addendum). For all these exchanges, I am grateful.

Reading the individual titles of the ten chapters may give the impression that they deal with disparate issues, but judging them by their content the reader should find that they all converge from different angles on the comprehensive issue of *communio*, its theological significance and its practical operation. *Communio* was the central theme of the Council. A good way of summing up its achievement may well be by saying: the Council Fathers made a profession of faith in the church of Christ as the *communio* of believers.

But to make a profession of faith in *communio* is one thing, to create it in the practical order is another. The Council lifted up the church to a new vision, or into a new field of vision, but it left little guidance for its implementation.

Now the community, the people led by the apostles' successors, has the task to build in a practical way the church as a sacred *communio*. We need an environment where Christians are increasingly free to use their gifts of grace and wisdom and where the Holy Spirit is not hampered by our rules.

We are still too close to the Council to sense and appreciate its full significance and potential impact. Through the ministry of Blessed John XXIII, the light and force of the Spirit touched the episcopate. Through the ministry of the Council, the same light and force are reaching and awakening the entire people of God. Such an irruption can upset our usual ways and habits. We need to adjust our eyes to the brilliance of the light, and our hearts to the demands of the force. Above all, we should hope in the mighty hand of God, who made a promise to Israel—a promise that remains valid for the new Israel that is the church:

> I will be as the dew to Israel;
> he shall blossom as the lily,
> he shall strike root as the poplar;
> his shoots shall spread out;
> his beauty shall be like the olive,
> and his fragrance like Lebanon.
> They shall return and dwell beneath my shadow,
> they shall flourish as a garden;
> they shall blossom as the vine,
> their fragrance shall be like the wine of Lebanon.
> (Hos 14:5-7)

Abbreviations

General

AAS	*Acta Apostolicae Sedis*
AS	*Apostolos suos*
ASS	*Acta Sanctae Sedis*
CDF	Congregation for the Doctrine of Faith
CIC	Code of Canon Law, 1983
DS	Denzinger-Shönmetzer
MP	*Motu Proprio*
PB	*Pastor Bonus*

Council Documents

DH	*Dignitatis humanae*
DV	*Dei verbum*
GS	*Gaudium et spes*
LG	*Lumen gentium*
OE	*Orientalium Ecclesiarum*
SC	*Sacrosanctum concilium*
UR	*Unitatis redintegratio*

In Praise of *Communio*
The Church in the Third Millennium

INTRODUCTION

The title of this chapter reflects an ambitious project. Its underlying question reaches into a future that is well beyond our horizon: *What is the church going to be in the third millennium?* Surely, we cannot see that far—not into the depth of a millennium.

The question, however, is deceptive. It is not about the future; it concerns the present. Let me reformulate it into two parts: As we perceive and experience various movements in the church today, do we find that some of them are portents of things to come? Do we find that they contain energies that are likely to shape the life of the community in the coming centuries?

Once our inquiry is put into such terms, it makes better sense. We are not guessing about the future but entering into a process of discovery concerning the present. The focus of our attention is not "what may happen" but what can be observed here and now. Our eyes are on the church of today.

CONTRASTING IMAGES

Today, the church is known through contrasting images.

On the one hand, it offers a strong image of well-being. The Roman Catholic community is recognized the world over; it has gained respect to a degree hardly seen before, especially through the activities of the papacy. The Holy See is strong. Outwardly, it is present and active in international assemblies, notwithstanding that its voice may be a cry in the wilderness; inwardly, the papacy has built up a tightly knit administrative organization that enables it to watch over the local churches and to intervene promptly with authority whenever it judges necessary.

On the other hand, too many local churches (too many for comfort) in various parts of the world are displaying the symptoms of deep-seated internal weaknesses. They celebrate the Eucharist less and less for lack of priests: the source of life is drying up. They are not allowed to celebrate the sacrament of forgiveness and healing in a renewed form (as the Council wished it and the faithful desire it), so that little healing takes place in an age when the reconciling power of grace is sorely needed. The numerous cases of abuse of minors have revealed an organization that lacks a vigorous "immune system" for self-protection; an infection can spread in the body before it is noticed and remedial action can be taken. In the West, people, especially young people, keep drifting away from the "institutional church" (as they say it), hardly realizing that to abandon the visible body is to lose touch with its invisible soul, the life-giving Spirit of Christ.

What is happening? The contrasting images cannot be explained in any other way than by the existence of conflicting currents in the community, in the minds and hearts of the people. The result is turbulence.

Indeed, "turbulent waters" may be the appropriate image to describe the internal state of the church. But let us make no mistake: by nature's law, there is no turbulence without an excess of energy—energy in the process of seeking equilibrium. Let us keep this parable in mind.[1]

If the turbulence is caused by colliding currents, where are they going? Where do they come from? One current seeks to uphold the order of a highly centralized administration; another seeks to create a new order according to the demands of communion.

One current has its origin in a distant past. A movement was initiated at the end of the eleventh century by Pope Gregory VII (1073–1085)[2] who liberated the Western church from an all-pervading secular influence. He performed a

---

1. One is reminded of the story of "the beginning" when chaos preceded creation. A remote analogy, to be sure, but the God of light and life is watching over our turbulence no less than at the time of the initial chaos.

2. For a detailed historical account of the origins of this centralizing policy, see Friedrich Kempf, "Primitiale und episcopal-synodale Struktur der Kirche vor der gregorianischen Reform," in *Archivium Historiae Pontificae* 16 (1978) 22–66. I quote the summary preceding the article (my translation from the original Latin *Summarium*):

> In antiquity the *episcopal* synodal structures were of great importance; they prevailed over the primitial structures. In the Carolingian and Ottonian times, however, they lost their strength while the primitial structures increasingly prevailed. [These changes] transformed the relations between bishops and metropolitans, between metropolitans and the Holy See, between the Holy See and the episcopate. There is no doubt that the Latin church by choosing its own way alienated itself from the Greek church, which much better preserved the episcopal synodal structures. This alienation went so far as to make their schism inevitable. (p. 2)

See also by Kempf, "Die Eingliederung der überdiözesanen Hierarchie in das Papalsystem des kanonischen Rechts von der gregorianischen Reform bis zu Innocenz III," in *Archivium Historiae Pontificae*, 18 (1980) 57–96. *Summarium* in translation:

much-needed and salutary operation, but by doing so, he also generated a policy in the Western church toward centralization. The trend received a strong impetus in the period of the Counter Reformation and reached its peak in the nineteenth, twentieth, and now twenty-first centuries. Not surprisingly, always in the West, the traditional Catholic doctrine of "communion" was gradually lost from sight and waned in practice. The Eastern churches remained more faithful to the ancient doctrine of synodality, and the two branches of the same tree kept growing in different directions. This "growing apart" from each other has probably contributed more to the mutual alienation of the two churches than the ill-conceived excommunication in 1054 of Michael Cerularius, Patriarch of Constantinople, by the impetuous and imprudent papal legate Humbert of Silva-Candida.

Thus, a new ideology and policy developed in the West from the end of the eleventh century through the second millennium. The church was increasingly perceived, in places high and low, as a rigidly hierarchical institution where divine gifts (except those conferred by the sacraments) descended on the community through the mediation of the popes, bishops, and clergy. Structures, laws, and practices were introduced accordingly, and doctrinal explanations were developed to justify them. All good things were seen as channeled from above. The superiors had the right to instruct and command; the subjects had the duty to listen and obey. No wonder then, that much of the God-given intelligence and energy "in the provinces" remained unused.[3]

The metropolitans, primates, and patriarchs who in early times enjoyed a relative autonomy, in the Code of Canon Law are listed among the persons whose power consists in a participation in the power of the Roman primacy. The Latin church alone holds this conception; it evolved gradually from the Carolingian times; it was forcefully applied by the popes of the Gregorian reform, then somewhat loosely by the contemporary canonists, more firmly by Gratian. Finally it was firmly established by the Decretists and the Decretalists, also by Innocent III, and it became prevalent for the following seven centuries. To this long historical period the ecclesiological doctrine of Vatican Council II put an end. (p. 57)

Kempf remarks in the conclusion of this second article: "In any case, the attitude [of the Latin church] towards the Eastern churches has substantially changed" (p. 96).

In a historical context it is easy to see that the reunion of the two churches does not depend on dialogues by select committees alone. The ecclesiastical communities and the faithful on both sides must enter into a vital process of "growing together," a process that is bound to take a long time before they can give each other the "kiss of peace" of full communion. (I thank professor Myriam Wijlens, University of Stuttgart, for drawing my attention to Kempf's statements.)

3. For another good summary of the development of this centralizing event, see Harold J. Berman, "Canon Law: The First Modern Western Legal System," in *Law and Revolution* (Cambridge: Harvard University Press, 1983), 199–224. He writes in substantial agreement with Kempf:

The other current is of recent origin. Pope John XXIII reversed the dynamics of centralization by calling an ecumenical council. He saw the need for a new order and for a far-reaching reform that he called *aggiornamento*, "updating," although he understood much of his project as a return to older traditions. Once the Council was in session, he did not impose on the bishops his own ideas, the prepared schemata, but he let the bishops take the initiative. They lived up to their providential mandate, and *from below* they gave a new direction to the church. They met in four sessions over four years, and through painful struggles, they gave a fresh vision to their people. They stated that the church was first and foremost a "communion," *communio*,[4] a union of persons in a unique sense—created by the Spirit of Christ. Thus Vatican Council II, in the Dogmatic Constitution on the Church (*Lumen gentium*), gave the people of God priority over the hierarchy.

VATICAN II: A SEMINAL COUNCIL

Vatican Council II was a *seminal* council, probably more so than any other in history. For this reason, to comprehend its spirit and to apply its "determinations" to the everyday life of the church may take longer than was the case for any other such event. The determinations need to unfold in the minds and hearts of the communities as well as of the individual Christians. They have set a new course for the church, a course that now causes turbulence but over the centuries will become an even flow.

Today the church is internally stressed and stretched, but we should not worry. If the impetus for the Council came from the Spirit, the Spirit will grant the needed strength for the people to cope with the troubles. The Council Fathers certainly believed that what they said and did "pleased the Holy Spirit," *placuit Spiritui sancto.*

Building on the Gregorian Reform, and especially on Gregory's Dictates of 1075, the canonists of the late twelfth and the thirteenth centuries attributed supreme governance (*imperium*) in the church to the pope. The pope was the head of the church, all other Christians were its limbs, its members. He had full authority (*plenitudo auctoritatis*) and full power (*plenitudo potestatis*). Although in practice his powers were limited—they increased only gradually, especially in the thirteenth and fourteenth centuries—nevertheless, in law, from the time of Gregory VII, the pope was the supreme legislator, the supreme administrator, the supreme judge. (p. 206)

4. To stress this vision and to emphasize that I am writing about a unique theological reality, I use the Latin term *communio*. Although it can be translated as "communion," its derivative in English does not have the rich content that the Latin has acquired in its Christian use.

With the same belief, we can read the signs of the times. There is the growing belief among the people that the church is a *communio* of persons—of *all* the persons. This *communio* cannot be identified with the pope, or the bishops, or the priests, or with any particular group.

WHAT IS *COMMUNIO*?

Although we often hear the expression "ecclesiology of *communio*," rarely are we given an insightful explanation of the theological reality to which it ultimately refers. Some who invoke it turn easily to secular models of unity, which may be useful but not enough. Others, after mentioning it, move hastily away from even trying to explain it—after all, it is a mystery, so they say. A mystery it is but not to the point of defeating any understanding.

Through faith, we discover *communio* in the inner life of God, who is one God in three persons. In God, there is unity in diversity, or diversity in unity. In this divine "model," mysterious as it is, we find the clue for achieving some comprehension of how the church is *communio*. In the church an organic unity exists among individual persons; they are bonded together. But how? The German theologian Heribert Mühlen described the church as "one person in many persons." The one Spirit of Christ dwells in many and holds them together.

Briefly but substantially, this is the theological reality of *communio*. All external manifestations of unity, such as collegiality and solidarity, flow from it. Among human beings, composed of spirit and matter, the internal and invisible mystery needs to manifest itself externally and visibly. One cannot exist without the other, not in this universe where the Word has become flesh.[5]

Hence the question: *In the church, what are, and what should be, the external structures and norms to express, to promote, and to sustain the internal bond of communio?* The answer may not come easily because our experience is confined to a highly centralized operation, but we should not be discouraged. If the Council mandates us to build *communio*, we have the means to do it. The first steps, however, must be taken in our imagination.[6]

---

5. In the Eastern tradition "synodality" has always been a dominant theme in ecclesiology, a theme honored in the frequent celebrations of synods; in the Latin tradition, due to the strong centralizing policies, it has not been given due attention.

6. For this method of "doing theology" by "imagination," I wish to give credit to Ghislain Lafont, O.S.B., of the Monastery of Pierre-qui-vire in France, former professor of theology at the Ateneo Sant'Anselmo in Rome; see his book *Imaginer l'Eglise catholique* (Paris: Cerf, 1995), available in English translation, *Imagining the Catholic Church* (Collegeville: Liturgical Press, 2000). The method is analogous to that of Einstein's "thought experiments"—a method as simple as it is productive. There is ample field for its application in theology and canon law.

IMAGINING

In the Catholic tradition, we have a splendid example of an "adventure in imagi-nation" in the famous work of St. Thomas, "The Best State of a Commonwealth and the New Island of Utopia." Utopia is, of course, a "noplace," or a place that existed only in More's fantasy. His aim was not to give a lesson in geography or history. As his publisher put it, the goal of the book was to provide "a truly golden handbook no less salutary than festive," *nec minus salutaris quam festivus.*[7]

This is what an adventure in imagination can accomplish: it can seek out life-giving features and celebrate them in a festive manner. The aim of such an approach is not to provide scholarly discourse or make an aggressive demand. It simply wants to throw light on what is fair, just, and beautiful—and then leave it at that, hoping that future generations will make a flight of fancy into life-giving reality.[8]

On a modest scale, imitating Sir Thomas, I intend that my presentation on the external features of the church as *communio* should be taken as a discourse that is "salutary and festive," as a piece "in praise of *communio*" with artistic liberties and fair excesses that are fitting for a solemn occasion.

THE UNIVERSAL *COMMUNIO* OF THE BAPTIZED BELIEVERS

The sacraments of initiation are visible signs of invisible events that only the eyes of faith can perceive; through them individual persons are assumed

---

7. See *Utopia by Thomas More*, ed. George Logan et al. (Cambridge: Cambridge University Press, 1999) 3.

The full title of the book deserves to be recorded: *De optimo reipublicae statu deque nova insula Utopia. Libellus vere aureus, nec minus salutaris quam festivus, clarissimi disertissimique viri THOMAE MORI inclitae civitatis Londinensis civis et Vicecomitis* (The Best State of the Commonwealth and the New Island of Utopia: A Truly Golden Handbook, no Less Beneficial than Festive, by the Most Distinguished and Eloquent Author THOMAS MORE, Citizen and Undersheriff of the Famous City of London).

In the spirit of Thomas More (who could doubt his wisdom and dedication to the church?) one could think of an enterprising canon law society that would call a convention *De optimo statu ecclesiae* ("The Best State of the Church") and afterward publish the proceedings under the title *Libellus vere aureus, nec minus salutaris quam festivus* ("A Truly Golden Handbook, no Less Beneficial than Festive")—covering conceivably all major topics in the Code. It sounds like a proposal fit for Utopia only, but it has proven its soundness and utility in the case of Sir Thomas. The task of such a convention would be to sow the good seed; the rest is the task of the Lord of the Harvest.

8. Indeed, Thomas discovered the life-giving nature of religious freedom and celebrated it on the pages of *Utopia.* His contemporaries paid no attention to his imagined new order; they were busy waging wars of religion. Only some four hundred years later, when Vatican Council II received his message, did his gentle vision become the hard policy of the church.

into the "body of Christ," a corporate body created by his Spirit. At this level there are no superiors and no inferiors: all are God's people. It is a *communio* of saints, as we profess in the Apostolic Creed, the ultimate source of the dignity and of the rights and duties of the Christian people.

This spiritual *communio* is an ontological reality and the origin and prototype of any other *communio* in the church. It is not a hypothesis; it is not an opinion. It belongs to the core of Catholic doctrine. In the Scriptures, the descent of the one Spirit on many persons proclaims it, and the parable of the vine and the branches illustrates it. In the East, the doctrine of "divinization" asserts it; in the West, the immense literature of the "indwelling Spirit" supports it. No matter what image we use, what events of salvation we refer to, the underlining ontological pattern is always the same: one person in many persons.

When it comes to creating structures and norms for communion, to the doctrine of *communio* we must turn, and from this belief we must start. The reason is obvious: If there is an internal union, it must become externally incarnate in the practical life of the church. If it is ignored, the practical forms of unity will be no more than organizational devices; useful they may be but not anchored in our faith.

Within this universal *communio* there is diversity enriching the whole body. The sacrament of orders creates a special bond among the clergy. The sacrament of matrimony holds spouses together. The charism of vocation to a consecrated form of life gives rise to religious institutes. They all are works of the Spirit. They all need visible structures and operating rules.

Vatican Council II, intending to stress the rule of the episcopate, described the church as a "hierarchical *communio*." It is a venerable expression since it comes from a council, but it requires explanation. "Hierarchical" is a predicate; *communio* is the subject. Hierarchical indicates that "by divine ordination" (cf. Council of Trent, Canon 6, *de ordine*) the organism is internally and externally structured. Within one *communio*, there are many smaller *communiones*. The Spirit gathers God's people into a diversified unity.

To say that the church is an "organically structured *communio*" would have been a more balanced expression.

COMMUNIO AMONG THE ORDAINED PERSONS: A PARTICULAR COMMUNIO WITHIN THE UNIVERSAL COMMUNIO

What is the sacrament of orders? What happens in an ordination? Normally, we think of ordination as the receiving of a gift through the imposition of hands with the appropriate prayers accompanying it. In our imagination we see this event as the symbol of a grace descending from above on the candidate. Such a perception reverses the true dynamics of the sacrament. Ordination is an act of the Spirit, who lifts up a person and incorporates him into the particular *communio* of the "servant shepherds" to serve *and* lead the community.

The *communio* among the ordained has its own structure: it includes bishops, presbyters, and deacons. But it is not a military organization where the highest in rank command and the others obey. They all have a common gift; they all must be of one mind and must work with one heart—they are a corporation. All canonical rules applicable to them must sustain and promote this unity. None of the three orders alone has the full intelligence and prudence needed for the proper care of a local church (a diocese). The bishop needs others to govern the diocese.

COMMUNIO IN THE LOCAL CHURCHES
BETWEEN THE BISHOP AND THE PRIESTS

In the invisible world of charisms, the bishop and the presbyters are members of the one organic "sacerdotal" body. Hence, there must be an effectively functioning *presbyterium* presided over by the bishop. To have a priests' council is not a concession; it is a theological necessity.

The promise of obedience that is demanded from the priest at the time of his ordination must be understood in the context of the existing sacramental *communio*: it is a one-sided expression of a two-sided covenant between the bishop and the priest. The bond of *communion* binds the bishop to a religious fidelity to his priests no less than it binds the priests to their bishop.

Although ordinarily we speak of the bishop and "his" priests, in truth, they are God's priests. They receive their "power to feed the flock" not from any human superior but directly from God through the sacrament of ordination. The role of the bishop is to insert the priests who are "anointed by the Spirit" into the visible structure of the diocese.[9]

COMMUNIO IN LOCAL CHURCHES BETWEEN THE BISHOP AND
PRIESTS ON THE ONE SIDE AND DEACONS ON THE OTHER SIDE

Although the diaconate has been restored recently, overall the deacons have not assumed their ancient tasks allotted to them in the early centuries. Their

---

9. There is a world of difference between saying that "the bishop empowers the priest to care for the people" and saying that "God empowers the priest, and the bishop designates the priest's place in the diocese." The former perception dominated the theology of priesthood before Vatican Council II; the latter is rooted in the theology of the Council. The practical attitude of the bishop toward his priests is determined by his theological vision. An analogous consideration applies to the relationship that exists between the pope and the bishops.

traditional function was twofold: to administer the physical and material possessions of the church (so that the bishops and presbyters would be free to proclaim the Word) and to take care of the orphans and the indigent, in more general terms, those whose lives were broken.

A full return to the early understanding of the deacons' task, to be agents of charity, would be desirable and it should not take away or diminish their participation in the liturgy; rather, it would incorporate them more intensely into the daily life of the community. Now we have many "permanent" deacons serving part time; after a full return we would have deacons ministering full time.

COMMUNIO AMONG THE BISHOPS: THE BISHOPS' COLLEGE

The theological opinions about the nature of the bishops' college are far from settled.[10] All agree that it is a structured *communio*: the pope is the head of the college, and he is a bishop like all the others, but he has the power of primacy over his brother bishops.

One school sees the pope as having two offices: one strictly personal, another corporate. He is the Vicar of Christ for the whole church and endowed with a plenitude of power, *and* he is the head of the episcopal college, playing an organic and indispensable role in the college. When an ecumenical council is in session, the pope participates in a corporate power—in a privileged way, as the head. But, should anything go wrong with the council's deliberations, he can simply assume his personal office of Vicar of Christ and dissolve the council.

Another school sees the college as an organic whole and its power indivisible. The pope has one office: he is Peter's successor and for that reason he is also the head of the college. In this opinion the promise of Christ to preserve the integrity of the church extends also to the integrity of the episcopal college.

Admittedly, we are dealing with a difficult issue, but the intense unity that is *communio* is hardly compatible with the theory of "two offices."[11]

---

10. Cf. "Preliminary Note" (*Nota praevia*) added as an appendix to the Dogmatic Constitution on the Church (LG).

11. The expression "Vicar of Christ" for the pope entered into use around the twelfth century; earlier "Vicar of Peter" was used. The title "Vicar of Christ" was born out of devotion and became hallowed through its constant usage by the faithful. It was never meant to be a precise theological or canonical statement; if it were taken literally it would raise serious problems. Vatican Council II tried to balance its one-sided use for the pope by repeatedly insisting that every bishop was a vicar of Christ in his diocese, which is essentially an assertion that there is one episcopate and all who received the sacrament share in it. The pope receives no higher gift in his ordination than the other bishops but he is given a much broader field for

This *communio* among the bishops generates in them a complex set of rights and duties. They together, with the pope presiding, must take care of the universal church. The principal instrument for this purpose has been, and remains, their meeting in an ecumenical council. It is the prime and full external manifestation of the internal "episcopal synodality" created and sustained by the Spirit.

Legitimate partial gatherings that do not break *communio* with the pope, however, are also authentic expressions of the bishops' unity. Historically, these gatherings have been a way of taking care of a group of local churches within the same cultural or political region. Right from the beginning the church honored such partial assemblies and listened to their voice. It follows that regional synods—or for that matter the episcopal conferences—have a life of their own and share in the power of the episcopal college.[12]

COMMUNIO BETWEEN THE CHURCH OF ROME AND THE OTHER CHURCHES: THE EXERCISE OF PRIMACY

The universal church is a structured *communio* of particular churches: a body composed of members that form a whole and operate as a whole. Never can a member be independent from the others. One of the churches, however—that of Rome— occupies a unique position, with proper rights and duties attached; it has primacy. It is the church of Peter and Paul; its bishop is the successor of Peter, mandated to confirm his brothers and sisters in faith and to guide the people on their way to salvation. The Spirit of Christ assists the church of Rome and its bishop in accomplishing this task.

In the course of nearly two thousand years the church of Rome and its bishop played their eminent role in safeguarding the Tradition. Over the centuries the faithful (in the Western church) increasingly recognized in them a special charism of fidelity that is not granted to others to the same degree. The definition of infallibility at the First Vatican Council was a fruit of this awareness, notwithstanding all the difficulties that it has engendered.

---

the exercise of his sacramental power. See "Titles, Papal" in *The Papacy: An Encyclopedia* (New York: Routledge, 2002) 3:1494–95.

12. The latest legislation concerning the episcopal conferences is contained in the Apostolic Letter by John Paul II, *Apostolos suos*, May 21, 1998: AAS 90 (1998) 641–58. Frederick McManus writes: ". . . this Apostolic Letter on 'the theological and juridical nature of episcopal conferences' insists very strongly upon the power of the individual bishops of particular churches and thus appears to situate the conferences in a somewhat secondary or ancillary role only—apart from their clearly pastoral, non binding decisions" (John P. Beal and others, eds., *New Commentary on the Code of Canon Law* [New York: Paulist Press, 2000] 22).

Yet, after Vatican Council II, the intense dialogues between the Roman Catholic *communio* and other churches and communities revealed a problem: widespread desire for change in the exercise of the Petrine ministry.

This aspiration is virtually unanimous in Christian communities separated from Rome, and it is quietly reinforced by Roman Catholic voices. Pope John Paul II heard them all, and in his encyclical "That They May Be One" (*Ut unum sint*), he recognized their concern. He responded by making an extraordinary request:

> I insistently pray [for] the Holy Spirit to shine his light upon us, enlightening all the Pastors and theologians of our churches that we may seek—together, of course—the forms in which this ministry may accomplish a service of love recognized by all concerned. . . . This is an immense task, which we cannot refuse and which I cannot carry out by myself. (95–96)

The pope's wish is marked by both certainty and uncertainty. He seems certain that some new forms for the "service of love" that he is called to provide are needed; his words signal that without significant changes his service may not be, or cannot be, perceived as a service of love. He is uncertain, however, how the established practice could be, or should be, changed; he realizes that the search for new ways is an immense task and that he cannot carry it out by himself. Yet, daunting as the task may be, "we cannot refuse it." He is asking for help. His cry is a beautiful affirmation of *communio*: all Christians are invited to be partners in a process of inquiry and discovery.

The pope's appeal did not fall on deaf ears: numerous authors responded in articles and books. Their works deserve attention but overall they did not provide adequate answers. Most, if not all, failed to realize the extent of the problem. They focused narrowly on the office of the pope and suggested various modifications of it, partly to make the papacy more attractive to the Christians outside the Roman *communio*, partly to bring the internal administration of the church into greater harmony with Vatican Council II.

But the papacy does not exist alone; it is an organic part of the Catholic *communio*. There is no way of finding "forms in which this ministry may accomplish a service of love recognized by all concerned" without a radical conversion of the whole Roman Catholic Church—communities and individuals—in their attitude toward the papacy. If the papacy ought to change, so must the faithful.[13] Reform can be obtained only through coordinated dialectical movements.

---

13. Some examples: the bishops who shun personal decisions and turn to Rome for guidance, *opportune et importune*, contribute as much to centralization as any Roman office can. Theologians who exalt the personal theological opinions of the pope into Catholic doctrine

It follows that reform in the exercise of primacy is possible only if it is balanced *by corresponding transformations within the community at large.* Such a transformation, however, might be more difficult to obtain than a new manner of exercising the papal office. It might be harder to change the expectations in the minds and hearts of the people at large (bishops included) than to introduce new administrative practices. Should the papacy be willing to relinquish some responsibilities to some lower organs, the lower units, mainly the bishops and their assemblies, must be competent, ready, and willing to take them. Conversions are needed all around.

In truth, the possible extent and the scope of such a reform are largely unexplored. For a long time, hostile attacks on the papacy compelled Catholic scholars to defend it; they had little time and energy to analyze the inner structures and the workings of the primacy and then suggest reforms. The last significant work on this topic may have been the letter of St. Bernard of Clairvaux, *De consideratione* (composed in 1150–1152), to Pope Eugene III (reigned 1145–1153) in which the saint called on the pope to decentralize his government.[14]

We are at a groundbreaking stage. For this reason, we ought to formulate our questions with utmost care. Our aim is to search for better balances without damaging vital forces.

RELIGIOUS COMMUNITIES IN A CHURCH OF *COMMUNIO*

I use the expression "religious communities" in a broad sense to cover the great variety of "institutes of consecrated life," "societies of apostolic life," and "secular institutes." Each forms a *communio* within larger *communiones* such as a diocese or the universal church. No matter what their structures and norms are, if they wish to flourish in the third millennium, they must appropriate and cultivate the essential elements of *communio.* They must do so within their own household and in their relationships with the local and universal church. For

---

(which he never intended) are destroying intellectual diversity in the church. The faithful who distort the respect due to "sacred pastors" (cf. Canon 212) into a cult of personality are hurting Christ's body—the church.

14. St. Bernard was an early supporter of the principle of subsidiarity, although he probably never heard of it. He writes to Pope Eugene III: "Your [superior] power, therefore, is not the only one that comes from God, there are intermediate and inferior powers. . . . You create a monster when, bypassing the hand, you make the finger depend on the head" (*Non tua ergo sola potestas a Domino; sunt et mediocres, sunt et inferiores . . . Monstrum facis, manui submovens, digitum facis pendere de capite*) [*De consideratione*, III:17]). From the context it is clear that St. Bernard considered the intermediate structures (e.g., metropolitans) as given and not to be absorbed by the papacy. See also "Eugene III" in *The Papacy: An Encyclopedia* (New York: Routledge, 2002) 1:533.

some, mainly those who have their origins in the first millennium, this will be easier: the Rule of Benedict is a guide for building small "cities of God" where *communio* reigns supreme. Orders founded in the second millennium, especially after the Council of Trent, may have to update their structures and manners of operation more extensively if they were designed in imitation of a highly centralized church. To seek the reforms needed is not infidelity to their charismatic founder; rather, it is fidelity to the ever-evolving charismatic life of the universal church. To cling to structures and norms that were historically conditioned and that the church is leaving behind would be to opt for stagnation and demise.

The ways and means of a renewed form of life ought to be created by the communities themselves. The potential for it is contained in the original charism, which ought to be a source of living water and not a set of rules carved into a lifeless rock. The Spirit who inspired the founders is not dead or absent. The Spirit's creative generosity is ever present. Excessive attachment to the ways and means of a remote past is a deadly apostasy from the life-giving present.

DOMESTIC CHURCHES

This study cannot be complete without paying due attention to the "domestic churches," that is, to the Christian families. Each one is a *communio*, and each is inserted into larger *communiones* that are the parishes, the dioceses, and the universal church. A modern fallacy is to regard families as private institutions: they are not. By nature, they are the building blocks of public communities.

Because our canonical tradition, formed mainly in the High Middle Ages under the impact of Roman law, regards marriage as a contract between spouses, it obscures the ecclesial character of the institution. The Eastern church places more emphasis on the ecclesial nature of the sacrament: it is akin to a consecration. The church through the officiating priest invests the couple with a sacred task: they should contribute to the growth of God's earthly kingdom by providing it with new members. Some historians even claim that the ceremony of the "crowning" of the couple had its origin in the ancient "imposition of hands": the spouses were "ordained" for public ministry in the church.

The Western church has come closer to the Eastern position by requiring in the celebration of the sacrament the active presence of a priest—at least in ordinary circumstances. Should we see such regulation as a doctrinal development?

COMMUNIO AND ECUMENISM

The restoration of the unity of Christian churches and communities is essentially a work of perfecting an already existing *communio* born from a common profession of faith and an identical baptism.

No universally applicable rule can be given as to how this unity should be brought to its fullness; it is a healing process. And healing is a complex art: It consists as much in building new relations as in removing old obstacles. It involves the conversion of minds and hearts of the communities and of the individual persons. At the starting point and throughout the process, we Catholics should keep in mind that our intent must not be "to bring back to Christ" a group of "schismatics" or "heretics" but to come together in faith, hope, and love. We must regard the "separated" communities as separated from us, not from Christ. They too surrendered to his Word; they too received his sacred rites. Such an approach will protect us from the fallacy that the healing process consists merely in coming to a common understanding through well-organized dialogues—indispensable as they are. An intellectual agreement not backed and sustained by the community at large cannot create unity: the aftermath of the Second Council of Lyon (1274) and the Council of Florence (ended in 1445) should prove that much abundantly. If today we hear that the dialogues among the churches are not producing their expected fruits, the reason is that the expectations were misplaced. The time has come for a more realistic approach: Christians praying together and practicing charity jointly can advance the union of churches as much as and more than the experts do through their dialogues.

A conception that places too much hope in the agreements among the leaders of the churches is an approach that is not based on historical experiences or on the understanding of the church as *communio*.

CONCLUSION: LOOKING INTO THE FUTURE

Vatican Council II ended in 1965 on the feast of the Immaculate Conception. After the solemn Mass at St. Peter's, Yves Congar, who contributed so much to the success of the Council, wrote in his diary:

> Today, the church is sent to the world: ad gentes, ad populos. *Incipiendo, non a Ierosolyma sed a Roma* [Starting not from Jerusalem but from Rome]. The Council will have an explosive force [*va éclater*] in the world. The moment of Pentecost that John XXIII has foretold has become a reality today.[15]

Decades later, we look back. Was Congar right? Has the Council become an explosive force among the nations? Do the people of the earth see the church coming to them in a new robe and speaking a new message?

It seems that the opposite has happened: while in some ways the church became more visible than ever, in other ways it has revealed immense internal weaknesses. The Council's achievement is hardly an explosive force in the

---

15. Yves Congar, *Mon Journal du Concile* (Paris: Cerf, 2002) 2:515 (my translation from the original French).

world. Did Congar misread the signs of the times and—in the exultation of the last session of the Council—fall into a false prophecy?

Not so. Congar saw rightly. His sight was sharp, his perception good. Yet as happened even to biblical prophets before him, while he saw the changes were coming, he did not see the distance in time before they would arrive. He saw a distant event as if it were imminent. In the exultation of singing the *Te Deum,* he failed to realize how much time would be needed to move from insights to practice—from vision to legislation. He was so enticed by the magnificence of the conciliar decisions that he did not notice the obstacles on the way to their implementation.

Today the conflicting dynamics that dominated the debates of the Council are active again in the universal church; the Council is replayed in the community at large. The currents from the second millennium favoring strong centralization are here and working; the currents promoting *communio* are strong and operating.

In our church of today, there is a fair amount of hidden dissent from the Council, mostly in the form of reinterpreting it to the point where it becomes insignificant and irrelevant. Yet, throughout the church, there is also an immense desire for the implementation of the Council's teaching and decisions.

How will it all end?

The church is in God's hand. But as we try to look into the future and ask *What is to come?* it is right and just to recall the statement first used at the apostolic council of Jerusalem: *placuit Spiritui sancto et nobis,* "for it has seemed good to the Holy Spirit and to us" (cf. Acts 15:28).

Ever since, the church peacefully believed that the determinations of the great councils pleased the Holy Spirit and that such determinations have an intrinsic force that cannot be lost in history. What God has initiated, God will bring to a good end. In God's own time, the Council will emerge in its entire splendor and with its radical exigencies that Yves Congar has so well perceived.

Gregory VII is remembered for having initiated a movement toward a strong centralized government. Perhaps in a millennium from now, John XXIII will be remembered for having changed the course of events and set the church on the path of *communio.* Blessed be his name.

Toward the end of the Council, when the outcome was already certain, Congar also wrote in his diary: *vidimus—videbimus mirabilia,* "we see—we shall see wonders!"[16] The correct answer to my original question, *What will the future hold?* should be: in God's own good time *vidimus—videbimus mirabilia,* "we see—we shall see wonders."

16. Ibid., 503.

2

Episcopal Conferences
Communio among the Bishops

On the feast of the Ascension in 1998, Pope John Paul II promulgated "on his own initiative," *motu proprio*, an Apostolic Letter titled "The Theological and Juridical Nature of Episcopal Conferences"; the opening words of the official Latin text are *Apostolos suos*.[1] At first sight, it may appear as a piece of highly technical proclamation with little relevance for the daily life of the believers; at closer examination, however, the *Motu Proprio* will reveal a far-reaching provision that is likely to shape the life of the church for a long time to come. After all, the bishops are the shepherds of the flock, and whatever they do rebounds on their charge, as we well know from Gospel stories.

The document can be understood, initially, as part of the great effort to translate the conciliar doctrine and ecclesiology into canonical language (see Apostolic Constitution *Sacrae disciplinae leges*).[2] Such move from theory to practice responds to a legitimate expectation: the task of the commentator-interpreter is to see how far the norms reflect the vision of the Council.

A cascade of propositions in the beginning introduces the central theme of the document, each of them affirming that the Lord himself intended to give a *collegial* character to the group of the twelve apostles: "The Lord Jesus constituted the apostles in the form of a college . . . The apostles were not chosen and sent by Jesus independently of one another, but rather as part of the group of the Twelve . . . They were sent by him, not individually, but two by two" (AS 1).

Strong references to the "college" of the apostles seem to suggest that the principal intent of the author is to assert a historical continuity initiating with the little band of the Twelve and stretching to the modern episcopal conferences. Thus, the individual apostles have died but the college continues to live.

The scope of my inquiry, therefore, is to see if the structures and norms promulgated and established by this *Motu Proprio* give the deserved and full

1. AAS 90 (1998) 641–58.
2. AAS 75 (1983-II) VII–XIV.

honor to the apostolic collegiality. My investigation falls into two parts, each responding to a distinct question. I will first ask if the provisions of *Apostolos suos* recognize in the episcopal conferences a genuine corporate power, rooted in the Spirit and expressed in collegial operation. As I shall come to a negative conclusion, I proceed and then ask what vision and legislation we need to ensure that the bishops gathered in conferences do not operate independently from each other, but like the apostles, they form a college (even if not the *full* college) and work collectively.

THE STRUCTURE AND THE NORMS OF OPERATION
OF THE EPISCOPAL CONFERENCES

Apostolos suos defines episcopal conferences as permanent organizations of the bishops of a certain territory. Individual bishops are brought together into an association through the instrumentality of a legal framework that is provided for them by the Holy See for the purposes of joint deliberations and concerted actions. Each member retains his rights and duties; none of his liberties or obligations is absorbed into a corporate power structure.

The Holy See constitutes the conferences canonically: it approves their statutes and controls their operations. We must assume, therefore, that the conferences *as corporations* are of human ecclesiastical origin. The source of their *corporate* power (as far as it exists) is in the papacy. This corporate power is merely juridical and not sacramental. The members operate jointly and not as an ontological unity having its own internal corporate strength.[3]

Conferences of bishops therefore are not corporations, *synodos*, or colleges of their own right in the proper sense of the term. In colloquial language, they are mere "associations" of individual bishops. When they have corporate power, it is a mere legal power; they have it in trust at the pleasure of the giver. As a result, all their corporate decisions and actions must conform to the intention of the principal.

All this is clearly stated in the *Motu Proprio*:

> The binding effect of the acts of the episcopal ministry jointly exercised within conferences of bishops and in communion with the Apostolic See derives from the fact that the latter has constituted the former and has entrusted to them, on

---

3. Vatican Council II was firm in asserting that bishops are not the delegates of the pope. But if the Holy See creates their conferences and has the exclusive right to invest them with collegiate power, it surely follows that much of their effective power is given to them by the same See; that is, their effective power originates in the office of the pope. Canonically the conference may have ordinary power; ontologically (and in common parlance) their power is delegated.

the basis of the sacred power of the individual bishops, specific areas of competence. (13)

This understanding of the episcopal conferences—*they are juridical entities created by the Holy See*—is the principle and foundation of the whole document. It gives the *Motu Proprio* an internal consistency in expounding the theory of the conferences and in regulating their operations. It defines both the attitude and policy of the Holy See toward the conferences and the individual bishops and the rights and duties of the conferences and individual bishops toward the Holy See. Further, it discourages the many bishops from thinking and acting *as a corporation*.

The juridical norms concluding the *Motu Proprio* reveal this position even more clearly; one rule virtually tells it all:

> In order that the doctrinal declarations of the conference of bishops . . . may constitute authentic magisterium and be published in the name of the conference itself, they must be unanimously approved by the bishops who are members or receive the *recognitio* (review) of the Apostolic See if approved in plenary assembly by at least two thirds of the bishops. (IV:1)[4]

The rule could not be clearer: the bishops can join their voices "in conference" but *the conference*, as such, has no voice.[5] Any decision is the sum of individual votes.

The Doctrine behind the Norms and Structures

The theological doctrine that has inspired the legal structures and norms states that *episcopal conferences have no corporate power.* In more theological

4. *Recognitio*, translated as "review," is a relatively new juridical formula in canon law, and ambivalent at that. In theory, the authority to act in the case is vested in a lower body (e.g., episcopal conference), but in practice no action can be taken by the lower agency until the intended act (declaration) is "reviewed" by a higher forum (the Holy See). The result is a legal anomaly—constitutionally someone has authority but cannot use it effectively.

5. In the present juridical order, episcopal conferences have a close affinity (built on near-identical patterns) with the Congregations of the Roman Curia.

In the legal order, both the Congregations and the conferences are administrative organs created by the authority of the pope. They have collective power as far as is granted to them by the pope; they exist at his pleasure.

In the theological order, the Roman Congregations and episcopal conferences are by their nature radically different. The Congregations are the executive organs of the papacy; they are entirely of human creation. The legitimate gatherings of bishops, full or partial, are manifestations of a divine design. The pope, therefore, has a duty to honor them and help them to obtain the necessary legal structures for their operations; cf. ". . . and when you have turned again, strengthen your brethren" (Luke 22:32).

terms, when groups of two or three (or more) bishops gather formally "in conference" together, we must not assume that there is any corporate energy in the body due to the assistance of the Spirit and prior to any legal structure. The saying of Jesus reported by Matthew—"For where two or three are gathered in my name, there am I in the midst of them" (18:20)—does not apply.

The text of *Apostolos suos* leaves no doubt about this position: "This territorially based exercise of the episcopal ministry [*as episcopal conferences are*] never takes on the collegial nature proper to the actions of the order of bishops as such" (12).

True, the document repeatedly affirms and upholds episcopal collegiality whenever the bishops meet in an ecumenical council or, although physically dispersed, their intentions and actions converge into a joint operation. They exercise "effective collegiality." What the *Motu Proprio* rejects throughout is a participation by conferences in this effective collegiality.[6]

Yet *Apostolos suos* admits that collegiality of a sort can be attributed to the conferences; the document calls it "affective collegiality." An inspiration for the use of this expression may have come from Vatican Council II. The Council mentions *collegialis affectus* twice (LG 23:52, AG 6:54); it is best translated as "an internal disposition to collegial action." The Council, however, does not use this expression in reference to episcopal conferences.

What is this "affective collegiality"? Is it a theological reality?

I suggest a theological thought experiment. What would happen if we applied the distinction between "effective" and "affective" to the exercise of the primacy? We know what "effective exercise" means: it was defined at Vatican Council I (and confirmed by Vatican Council II) as direct, immediate, and ordinary jurisdiction. But what could be the "affective exercise" of the primacy? Paternal disposition? Inspiring discourses? Encouraging counseling? Whatever it could be, it would not be the exercise of primacy with jurisdiction. So it is with collegiality: affective collegiality is not real collegiality.

The doctrinal position of *Apostolos suos* can be summed up in this way: the conferences of bishops do not partake at all of the collegial power of the

---

6. The official position of the Holy See (as far as we can ascertain it) is that effective collegiality does not exist outside of an ecumenical council; in other words, the collegial power of the bishops operates either fully or not at all.

This interpretation of collegiality is hardly compatible with the events and decisions of Vatican Council II. It is well known that the debate on collegiality was one of the fiercest of the Council: all understood that much more was at stake than to affirm that collegiality is fully operative at an ecumenical council—a doctrine commonly and peacefully accepted by all Catholics before the Council.

episcopate; however, they should be animated by a "collegial spirit," which is no more than a disposition to deliberate and to act jointly.[7]

Testing the Theory with Questions

The best way of testing a theory is to put it into a crucible of questions. A well-grounded position has nothing to fear from questions: the more searching they are, the stronger the truth will shine. An ill-construed hypothesis will reveal its weakness, step-by-step, as the questions accumulate.

1. Does the document recognize any authentic corporate power in the conferences?

The answer is in the negative: *Apostolos suos* does not recognize the theological reality of a corporate power in legitimate but partial gatherings of the bishops. It admits only the power of the local bishop within his diocese and the power of the episcopal college fully activated either in an ecumenical council or in dispersion but acting together. Between these two "extremes," there is no room for partial assemblies of bishops exercising effective corporate power.

It is difficult to see why there could not be a gradual growth in the corporate power of the episcopate from the individual bishop to the full college. Should we assume that the Spirit assists the bishops in their dioceses and at ecumenical councils (or the equivalent of it in dispersion) but not in their partial gatherings such as conferences? No plausible theological reason can be given for asserting such a restriction of the assistance of the Spirit.

2. Does Apostolos suos *accept a real analogy between particular synods and episcopal conferences?*

It does not. Although, interestingly, it does not hesitate to affirm that in the history of the church particular councils were indeed invested with power and had the assistance of the Spirit (3). But then it draws a distinction between these councils and the conferences: "unlike councils, [conferences have] a stable and permanent character" (4). In this context, this "stable and permanent character" appears as the reason for denying the conferences any participation in the power of the college. The argument is at best puzzling; at worst it appears absurd. Why should the Spirit deny assistance to an assembly of bishops because it has a "stable and permanent character"?

---

7. The way *Apostolos suos* conceives an episcopal conference has a similarity with the institution of *societas* of classical Roman law. The group as such has little power; should one member drop out, the *societas* collapses. Should one member of a conference dissent in a doctrinal decision, the consensus of the rest is of no consequence.

The Fathers of Vatican Council II in their Decree on the Pastoral Office of Bishops handled "Synods, Councils, and especially Episcopal Conferences" under one heading. Thus, they did not assume sharp differences among them. We find a similar approach in the new Code of Canon Law:

> Although the bishops who are in communion with the head and members of the college, whether individually or joined together in conferences of bishops or in particular councils, do not possess infallibility in teaching, they are authentic teachers and instructors of the faith for the Christian faithful entrusted to their care; the Christian faithful are bound to adhere with religious submission of mind to the authentic magisterium of their bishops. (Canon 753)

Interestingly, this canon recognizes the magisterium of bishops "joined together in conferences"—without insisting on unanimity on any issue.

3. Does the Motu Proprio *acknowledge a real analogy between the conferences in the Latin church and the permanent synods traditional in the Eastern church?*

This question could have been formulated in a different way: Is there a horizontal continuity in belief with our sister churches of the East? Such formulation would have brought the ecumenical aspect of the issue to the forefront. The substance of our faith is the same; there should be one doctrine throughout the Eastern Orthodox churches and the Western church.

No such ecumenical stance is patent in the document, although the very "stable and permanent" character of the conferences could have suggested one since also the synods of the Eastern churches are stable and permanent. If we see (as we do) their nature and practice as authentic expressions of Christian tradition, it would have been a gracious gesture toward unity to revive the same tradition in the West. Surely, when our sister churches see that the Latin church recognizes the power of the Spirit in the conferences, as they do in their synods, they will feel closer to us. Moreover, any movement toward more collegial governments would attract the sympathy of the Protestant communities as well.

4. Does Apostolos suos *attribute to the episcopal conferences any corporate power to teach?*

It does not; it does the opposite, since a conference must not issue any doctrinal declaration unless each member agrees to it or the Holy See approves of it. Such a requirement makes any serious teaching virtually impossible because in the practical order such unanimity cannot be expected.

It could be argued that the purpose of the rule is to preserve the unity of doctrine. In reality, however, it is more likely to hinder the proclamation of the Gospel and extinguish the diversity of theologies. For a conference to be alive, it must carry on intense dialogues among its members, but no dialogue is possible without divergent viewpoints that lead to a better understanding of the problem under debate. The final resolution is hardly ever unanimity; it consists in a healthy convergence of various positions. This has been very much the manner of operation of all general and particular councils.

With the burden of the present requirement, many conferences may be confronted with a choice between two disagreeable alternatives. One is to abandon any ambition to teach, knowing that unanimity (especially in a larger group) is virtually impossible; another is to keep sending their intended doctrinal statements for review to Rome, in which case they should either accept to be muted or submit themselves to unpredictable delays while the Roman offices work on their projects. The ultimate result in both cases is that the lively and timely proclamation of the Gospel with the collective authority of the successors of the apostles becomes nearly impossible.

5. This last question goes to the heart of the matter. *Although* Apostolos suos *seems to reject any innate corporate power (synodality) in the conferences, it affirms that they operate collegially. What is the meaning of such a collegiality?*

Apostolos suos does indeed affirm some corporate power in the conferences, but it sees—and defines—this power as purely legal. Therefore, collegiality means an organizational structure that holds the bishops together and not an expression of an internal corporate strength.

The consequences are far reaching. Although within the same cultural region it is a theological necessity for the bishops to deliberate and decide together (otherwise their contribution to the church's diversity remains ineffective), the moment they wish to work as a collective body, they can do so only as an institution created by the Holy See. While it is Catholic doctrine that individual bishops are not delegates of the Holy See, their conferences exist and operate on the basis of a power granted by the Holy See.[8]

Catholicity means both unity and diversity. Vatican Council II speaks of the dynamic balance between the two: "In virtue of this catholicity each part contributes its own gifts to other parts and to the entire church, so that the whole and each of the parts are strengthened by the common sharing of all things and by the common effort to achieve fullness in unity" (LG 13).

The principle of unity is the pope. The representatives of diversity are the bishops. Should the bishops fail in their task, the whole church would be weakened—including the papacy.

---

8. *Apostolos suos* does not seem to take sufficient notice that bishops are ordained into a church-wide college and consequently have a duty of care for the universal church.

To conclude the test: the theology that has inspired *Apostolos suos* does not blend harmoniously into our tradition. When it is tested in the crucible of legitimate questions, it fails to provide satisfactory answers; worse still, it reveals new and disturbing problems.

Further arguments about laws and ordinances are not likely to lead very far. We must move into a broader horizon and find a new theological vision; that is, we ought to move to a higher viewpoint and reorder our structures and norms.

Our tradition is rich enough to help us.

NEW HORIZON, NEW STRUCTURES

First I shall search for a fresh theological vision and then for appropriate legal structures and norms to express the scope of that vision. In the first exercise, "faith is seeking understanding," *fides quaerens intellectum*; in the second "faith is seeking action," *fides quaerens actionem*. There should be a harmonious sequence between the two.

Faith Seeking Understanding

Inspiration for the vision that I invoke comes from the writings of St. Paul the Apostle: ". . . all of us . . . have been baptized into Christ Jesus . . ." (Rom 6:3), he teaches. Through our baptism we, his readers, have been organically inserted into Christ's body—the church. Christ's Spirit animates this body. The one Spirit is the living bond among many persons and the principle of life for them and their community.

Paul's understanding of the church attracted the Fathers of Vatican Council II and led them to give a new impetus to an "ecclesiology of *communio*." *Have no fear* was their message, because no Christian is ever alone. Each person is an integral part of a body where all the organs work together for the good of the whole: one body, one soul. Because of this, when disciples meet for a sacred purpose in the name of Jesus, the result is not an accidental juxtaposition of individuals but a new manifestation of an organic life arising from the union of the members. A gathering of Christians can never be a mere "joint operation" of single human beings; the Spirit holds the group together. Once they are united, they participate in a preexisting power of the Spirit that makes their prayer more effective and their good work more pleasing to God. This is the theological reality of *communio*. Keeping this mystery in mind, we can grasp the depth and breadth of the saying of Jesus reported by Matthew. When the disciples come together Jesus will reward them with his presence: "For where two or three are gathered in my name, there am I in the midst of them" (18:20).

As the church is a *communio*, so is the body of the bishops. Ordination is not an exclusively personal gift that the recipient takes home and keeps as a treasure in his diocese: it is a sacramental act of the risen Christ that incorporates the new pastor into the organic body of the episcopal college—even before he receives his assignment from the pope. *Apostolos suos* reminds us that "the apostles were not chosen and sent by Jesus independently of one another, but rather as part of the group of Twelve" and that on the day of Pentecost they were "filled with a new vitality which comes from the Paraclete" (1).

For this reason, their successors, the bishops, are "part of an undivided body . . . the reality of this communion" (3). Now, it is inconceivable that when several bishops gather for a sacred purpose in the name of Jesus, in fulfillment of their mission, Christ would not honor them with his special presence, and that his presence would not be a source of collective strength and corporate energy in their assembly. They are not just individuals placed side by side: they are already "part of an undivided body" held together by the Spirit. They are many persons in one Person, animated by one vital Principle.

The entire people of God sensed this, from the earliest times, "with that supernatural sense of the faith" (LG 12) that only the Spirit can give. The people revered and obeyed particular councils, even before the great synod of Nicea. They have continued to do so ever since. Also, the bishops in various assemblies have continued to convey to the faithful that they believed in a special presence of the Spirit within their assemblies.[9]

In this wholesome theological vision we see the episcopal conferences integrated into the Christian community—all rooted in the presence and work of the Spirit. Whenever and wherever a number of bishops gather in the legitimate exercise of their office of teaching, sanctifying, and governing, and in communion with the successor of Peter and their brother bishops, they participate in the intense energy of the Spirit that has been promised to Christians who pray and work together. Of course, "participation" does not mean "totality," such as infallibility in teaching or some supreme prudence in deciding practical matters, but it means genuine taking part in the assistance and guidance of the Spirit, a theological reality not measurable by quantitative criteria.[10]

---

9. A testimony from silence has its own validity: no bishops' synod, council, or, for that matter, conference ever ventured to say that their gathering is a mere "joining of the forces of individual bishops"—such a way of thinking would have been totally alien to them.

10. Jérôme Hamer, O.P., a theologian of collegiality and a close witness of the intention of Vatican Council II, later Archbishop Secretary of the Congregation for the Doctrine of Faith, and Cardinal Prefect of the Congregation for the Institute of Consecrated Life, wrote in 1963 ("Les conférences épiscopales, exercice de la collégialité," in *Nouvelle Revue Théologique* (1963) 966–69, my translation):

This doctrine of *limited participation* in the full power of the college by an assembly that is part of that college is not without sound parallel. The day-to-day teaching and governing activities of the pope are explained with the help of the theory of "partial use of full power." For instance, canon law demands due respect, *obsequium*, for any official, though fallible, teaching of the pope (see Canon 752), although such a teaching is only a restrained and partial manifestation of the pope's full teaching authority. Interestingly, the Congregation for the Doctrine of Faith—Holy Office, by its earlier name—sometimes refers to its own work as "not without the assistance of the Spirit"; it is a curiously cautious reference to the doctrine of participation.[11]

Seeking Harmony

Scientists like to assume that there is hidden simplicity and harmony in the operation of nature—notwithstanding any principle of "uncertainty." For this reason, after finding a puzzle, they look first for a theory that is elegant in its simplicity. I wish to follow the same method because, if it works in natural sciences, it should work even better in theology. We can assume that simplicity and harmony reign in God's household.

I have already proposed the theory of internal and spiritual synodality in the Spirit of which collegiality is the external and legal expression. Now it is fair to subject it to the same scrutiny that I used to examine the validity of the legal approach that inspired *Apostolos suos*.

By its own nature, the episcopal collegiality consists not only in a universal exercise, covering the entire world, as for instance in the case of an ecumenical council, but also in an exercise more limited, covering a region. (968)

There are not two episcopal collegialities, one practiced at a universal level and another manifest at a regional level. There is only one that has modalities of infinite variety. This is the one collegiality of the episcopal body with the pope at the summit . . .

In sum: the episcopal conferences, demanded by the evolution of the world, are not just a practical provision, but they are a possible expression and an appropriate manifestation of the solidarity of the episcopal body of divine law in the church of Christ. (969)

As far as I can see, Hamer's view is very similar to (if not identical with) the vision I am proposing here.

11. The caution is justified: the teaching authority of the pope cannot be delegated because it is a "power to witness" with the assistance of the Spirit. Not even the pope can delegate the Spirit's assistance.

*1. Does the theory of synodality affirm authentic corporate power
in the conferences?*

Yes, it does. It affirms that legitimate gatherings of bishops are endowed
with a corporate power through the presence of the Spirit who ordained the
individual persons into a preexisting corporate unity established by Christ
among the apostles. This corporate unity has endured throughout history;
synodality among the successors of the apostles was never terminated. It continues to exist and operate today, fully when an ecumenical council is in session,
partially when a lesser assembly is in operation. The privileged assistance of
the Spirit does not emerge suddenly (and quasi-magically) when the whole
communio is called to action but gently and discreetly accompanies the "parts
of the body" in every one of their movements. The intensity of the Spirit's assistance in a partial gathering is less than what it would be in an ecumenical
council, as the intensity of the Spirit's support to the pope is less when he is
composing an exhortation than when he is defining a point of doctrine.

*2. Does the synodal theory accept a real analogy between particular synods
and episcopal conferences?*

Yes, it upholds a close analogy between particular synods and conferences.
Both are gatherings of bishops for the collective exercise of their duty. There
is no dissimilarity so significant that it would compel us to deny the existence
of a spiritual corporate power to the conferences while attributing it to particular synods.

*3. Does the synodal theory acknowledge a real analogy between the conferences in
the Latin church and the permanent synods traditional in the Eastern churches?*

It does, and by doing so it fosters the movement toward unity with the
Orthodox churches. True, episcopal conferences are not exactly the same as
patriarchal or metropolitan synods; yet the two *as theological realities* are close
to each other. By acknowledging a synodal power of the conferences as the
source and foundation of their collegial structure, the Latin church would come
close to the Orthodox tradition, a move that would facilitate the cause of reunion. Patriarch Bartholomew in 2008, in his address to the Synod of Bishops,
stated:

> It is well known that the Orthodox Church attaches to the Synodical system
> fundamental ecclesiological importance. Together with primacy, synodality
> constitutes the backbone of the Church's government and organization. As our
> Joint International Commission on the Theological Dialogue between our
> Churches expressed it in the Ravenna document, this interdependence between
> synodality and primacy runs through all levels of the Church's life: local, regional

and universal. Therefore, in having today the privilege to address Your Synod our hopes are raised that the day will come when our two churches will fully converge on the role of primacy and synodality in the Church's life.[12]

Moreover, any change toward some type of synodality in the Roman Catholic Church would command the sympathetic attention of the communities of the Reformation.[13]

4. Does the synodal theory support the episcopal conferences' corporate power to teach?

Yes. The theory upholds a venerable tradition that goes back to the pre-Nicean church, namely, the belief that local synods have teaching power. Some of those early synods were probably meeting with no less regularity than modern conferences. Of course, whatever happened in the past, today we should be aware that conferences could (and possibly would) produce doctrinal statements that are in need of completion or correction, or ordinances that demand prudent revision. The universal church, however, is healthy enough to deal with such imperfections. Conceivable dangers and possible mistakes are not good counsels for universal legislation. The overriding purpose of our laws should be to facilitate the proclamation of the Gospel. In our age, marked by speed, it is far more important to have good provisions for an effective and speedy evangelization by the conferences than to set up safeguards that can paralyze them and prevent them from fulfilling their mission. An excessive fear of a mistake may lead to the silencing of the truth.

12. The Patriarch spoke in English; text published in *Synodus Episcoporum Bulletino* 30, Vatican City, October 10, 2008. The Patriarch's discourse provides salutary food for thought for everyone in the Catholic Church. In a courteous and delicate way he affirms that a system of synodal government is a condition for reunion. Further he names synodality and primacy as the two interdependent supporting structures of the government at every level. Clearly, such interdependency cannot exist if synodality is merely "affective" and primacy is "effective." Further, to be a backbone of the church's government and administration, such interdependency must operate on all levels, local, regional, and universal. Note also that synodality in the Orthodox tradition means an internal unity, *communio*, created and sustained by the Spirit; a visible and legally structured collegiality cannot be but an external expression of an internal spiritual reality.

13. The tradition, *paradosis*, as it has been kept alive in our sister churches in the East, can help us further to understand the nature of the regional gatherings of the bishops of the Roman communion; we share the same faith. The Eastern churches have an uninterrupted tradition of synodal government that is stable and permanent. Should we deny that their synods have true collegial power, that their synods gather in "the Spirit"? Surely not. If we do not deny it to them, why do we deny it to ourselves? And when we deny this to ourselves, are we not condemning them? After all, we are one church in "orthodox faith," and the Spirit operates in the same way in the two branches.

5. The last question goes to the heart of the matter. *Does the synodal theory confess and honor effective collegiality in the conferences?*

It does, and it understands this effective collegiality as a partial manifestation of the synodal power of the entire episcopal body. It is authentic only when it is practiced in full communion with the head and the rest of the members. When it fulfills all the requirements for a correct process, it makes an indispensable contribution to the integrity of the church's social body: it upholds unity and promotes diversity.

The scrutiny of the synodal theory is now concluded and shows that this theological position is wholesome and elegant in its simplicity when compared with the theological position behind the rules of *Apostolos suos.*

Further, let the reader ponder whether *Apostolos suos* is internally consistent and coherent. First, in its introductory paragraphs it attributes what can be only effective collegiality to the apostles even when they are sent two by two. Then it states (following Vatican Council II, LG 22) that the bishops through their consecration are united among themselves in the same way, "*pari ratione . . . inter se coniunguntur*" (2). But at the end, it allows only affective collegiality to the conferences, which is certainly not the same *pari ratione* that the apostles had; rather, it is the denial of what they possessed.

Uncreated Spirit: Created Energy

In the church, the source of all power is in the living Spirit: "we believe in the Holy Spirit, the Lord, the giver of life." The presence of the uncreated Spirit in God's people is like burning fire: it radiates light and strength throughout the whole body. The Spirit infuses created energy into the whole organism; no member, head, limb, or "limbs united," can move without it.

Throughout the history of the church, this energy has sustained beliefs and operations of the whole community, to the point that "the whole body of the faithful who have received an anointing which comes from the Holy One cannot be mistaken in belief" (LG 12) and that many, known to God alone, have had the strength to be martyrs for their faith.

This same energy brought together the apostles and brings together the bishops. It gives light and strength to them as needed, so that they can proclaim with clarity the apostolic tradition and witness with strength God's love for the human family. According to historical circumstances, opportunities, and needs, such "proclaiming and witnessing" may take place when the bishops are assembled in a council, or when their judgments converge into a common profession of faith, or when the head of the college, the pope, defines the faith of the whole people of God. Let us recall: there is no college without its head, and there is no head without its body. This ontological bond is so strong that, were it broken, the life would leave the college.

The uncreated energy of the Spirit is always present and active in the entire church, just as the soul is always present and active in every part of the human body. For this reason, when a group of the faithful meet for a sacred purpose, energy received from the Spirit wells up in that group: "there am I in the midst of them," says the Lord (Matt 18:20). Even more so, when the successors of the apostles meet, in synods, councils, or conferences, they are heirs to a privileged situation and beneficiaries of a presence and assistance that the Spirit alone can give and that we can never measure. All we know is that the gift is there. Legislation by the Holy See can and should set structures and norms for a legitimate meeting. However, no pontifical law or delegation can be the source of divine energy, nor can the appointment of a bishop to a particular see by the pope give the sacrament of order.

This is, in substance, the theological vision I propose; practical norms should follow accordingly. Let the reader be the judge and answer the question: is this vision about the power of the conferences in harmony with the power that the church possesses?

Faith Seeking Action

Faith seeks the understanding of the mysteries. When it reaches understanding, then with the same energy, faith seeks action, *fides quaerit actionem*— all in one single uninterrupted movement. It is fair and just, therefore, to ask what structures and norms should flow from the doctrinal image contemplated. It is not a question of trying to craft precise rules; it is an attempt to find some guiding principles for new legislation.

The operational norms of episcopal conferences must have two dimensions: they must preserve and promote the unity of the whole college under the presidency of Peter, and they must give scope to the local conferences to work to the full measure of their capacity. The power of the papacy should not impede the growth of a strong episcopacy: the church needs conferences with original insights and creative initiatives. On the other hand, the power of the episcopacy should not in any way harm or destroy unity or fragment the church. Restraint is necessary on both sides. Structures and norms should prevent the encroachment of one institution on the other.

How could the present structures and norms be changed to obtain and sustain such a delicate balance? To begin, the universal law should acknowledge the fundamental right and duty of bishops, flowing from their ordination, to assemble for pastoral purposes. This must not be a concession from the Holy See; it can be only an affirmation of what exists by divine institution.

The universal law can and should give norms for this recognition; it should be a declaration of *communio* on the part of the pope, the head of the college. The Holy See can and should retain the ultimate supervisory authority over the conferences but more in the manner of a court of appeal (which is very traditional) than in the way of an ever-present director in all their actions.

The law itself should also encourage the conferences to work for the healthy blending of the Gospel message and the local culture. This is particularly important for the young churches in various continents.

The crippling rule of unanimity for doctrinal proclamation should be removed. It paralyzes the conferences, especially the larger ones. They are hampered in their effort to "let faith seek understanding," since no matter how sound a penetrating new insight is, the rule compels the whole conference to wait until the slowest of the bishops understands it. They all are impeded in evangelization because they are not allowed to speak until everyone agrees to the very same words, or until an office in Rome grants approval.

CONCLUSION

The ancient Greeks used the term *aletheia* for "truth." Analytically, the word in its roots signifies something that is not hidden, an object that reveals itself. On careful analysis, the structures and norms recently imposed by the Holy See on the episcopal conferences do not conceal but rather reveal a deep theological imbalance in the life of the church: the function of the episcopate has been taken over to a great extent by the primacy. This is the truth.

If this trend continues, the church will have an enfeebled episcopate. Yet in our modern world, no bishop can be pastorally effective alone. He must work with his brother bishops within the same cultural territory. The only institutions for such common work, apart from rare particular synods, are the conferences. But the moment they find themselves "in conference," in their common deliberations and decisions (at least in the practical order), they find themselves directed and controlled by the offices of the Holy See.

Further, no institution can remain effective unless it has living space and freedom within it to be creative. If such conditions are not given, it will stagnate.

In his far-reaching encyclical on ecumenism, "That They May Be One" (*Ut unum sint*), John Paul II asks "all the pastors and theologians of our churches" to seek with him, "together, of course," how the pope's ministry "may accomplish a service of love recognized by all concerned" (95). Clearly, the answer cannot but be complex and difficult. Yet it would be wrong to evade the summons that comes to us from the Vicar of Peter and that echoes the summons of Vatican Council II for ongoing reform.

A significant step toward the renewal of the Petrine ministry would be the strengthening of the episcopate, according to the mandate given to Peter: "Simon, Simon, behold . . . strengthen your brethren," said the Lord (Luke 22:31-32). Such "strengthening" in the concrete order would speak loudly. It would be noted, welcomed, and admired, not only in our Catholic community, but also throughout the world of Christian believers. Spiritually, it would take us closer to many of them. It would also revive some of our venerable traditions.

Restoring to the bishops the autonomy that is their birthright (a right flowing from their ordination) would open an immense source of fresh insights and creative initiatives for the salvation of the world. In order for the Good News to be received, it must blend into ". . . all that is good and right and true . . ."(Eph 5:9) within the local culture. No Roman office can lead such developments. The local episcopate must do it—as the bishops did it many times in past centuries. Was this not the work of Augustine in England? Of Boniface in Germany? Of Cyril and Methodius in the immense regions of the Slav nations? Of Patrick in Ireland?

Let me close these reflections with a story that can never be verified but that carries a weighty message. It is well known that during the first session of Vatican Council II a crisis developed. The bishops turned away from the voluminous drafts prepared mostly under the direction of the offices of the Holy See. The Fathers were given a stale drink to taste; they wanted new wine. Pope John XXIII understood them and let them have their way: he authorized new committees and was willing to receive new texts. Then a group of concerned officials from the Roman Curia, shocked by these events, visited the pope and warned him that if he gave that much freedom to the bishops, they would run away with his Council. Should that happen, the pope would lose control. A disaster would be bound to follow. The pope's answer was, so the story goes, "The bishops, too, have the Spirit."

Such faith in the episcopate is really the first step toward an ongoing reform of the episcopal conferences and perhaps toward a substantial renewal of the Petrine ministry. Once this faith is here, hope and love can do the rest.

A Doctrinal Note: Diversity by Divine Intent

A pioneering study about the theological nature of the episcopal conferences is *The Episcopate and the Primacy* in the *Quaestiones disputatae* series by Karl Rahner and Joseph Ratzinger, published in its original German in 1961. It contains three essays, one by Ratzinger and two by Rahner. Several of the authors' insights had an impact on the deliberations on collegiality at Vatican Council II. Chapter 3 by Rahner, "On the Divine Right of the Episcopate," remains particularly relevant. Its point is that by divine right there ought to be unity and diversity in the church, and that while the papacy is the principle of unity, the episcopal college is the representative and guardian of diversity. The importance of the issue justifies a somewhat lengthy quote:

> The unity of the church as a whole demands, of course, a certain homogeneity among her members, which is either presupposed or when lacking must be created. . . . Yet, pluralism in the church is not merely something unavoidable or something to overcome but something requiring encouragement and protection. . . .
>
> This legitimate and necessary pluralism in the church is not only pluralism of the individual members, but also of the larger groups of local churches, of countries and peoples, especially since these too, as such, have a "vocation" to the light of the Gospel. It would thus be preposterous to think, for example, that the existence of the Oriental churches, with their no-Latin rites, their own ecclesiastical law and theology, their own spirituality and piety, etc., is only tolerated by an indulgent Rome, as though Rome, for purely tactical reasons had resigned itself to the virtually inevitable, as though an absolute uniformity of law, liturgy, etc., were really the ideal. Such a theory, if taken seriously, would be outright heresy. Obviously it is impossible to lay down once and for all exact, material norms for the proper proportion between necessary homogeneity and pluralism *iuris divini* [by divine law]. But in principle the church also has the right and duty to encourage and to develop a genuine pluralism in all spheres of her existence and activity, in the manner appropriate to each sphere.
>
> Neither in practice nor ideally is the church a systematically administered unitary state.[14]

In the midst of the massive amount of theological and canonical information concerning the episcopal conferences, it is easy to lose sight of a central issue, which is diversity in the church. By divine law, the Christian community must have its unity; by the same divine law, it must have diversity. This is what Rahner is stressing; this is the principal meaning of this chapter. Once this doctrine of diversity is accepted as part of our Catholic heritage, the practical consequences are far reaching: diversity must be established, sustained, and nourished just as much as unity. Today the unity of the Catholic Church is firmly established. The people rally around the successor of Peter with devotion and respect. At the same time, there is a need for a greater diversity than our present structures and norms would allow.

Further, there cannot be successful evangelization without respect for diversity. All human beings are God's creatures; all nations are waiting for the

---

14. Karl Rahner and Joseph Ratzinger, *The Episcopate and the Primacy* (New York: Herder and Herder, 1962) 105–6.

Good News of redemption. But, no matter how good the message may be, it will not touch the minds and the hearts of the people unless it blends with the culture in which it seeks incarnation. In this process, the bishops of the region ought to be the principal agents in proclaiming the old truth in a new language and communicating the ancient tradition through fresh symbols. However, they cannot accomplish this divine task without due autonomy.

Finally, there are the separated Christian churches and communities: they are waiting, watching, and praying for the coming of the one church of Christ. Full reunion may be still far away, but by the grace of God we are making progress. However, we all, Catholics and non-Catholics, know and understand that full unity will not be possible without allowance for a great deal of diversity among the particular churches. This diversity will manifest itself in rights, structures, and emphases—as it happened in the early centuries. To guide such delicate and sensitive developments we need local leaders: the bishops and their conferences. They, in their turn, in order to be creative, "for the sake of the Gospel" need all the autonomy that divine law permits and that divine mission demands.

Addendum: Note on a Debate

The central insight in this chapter is that sacramental episcopal ordination is the entry into a particular *communio, synodos,* created and sustained by the Spirit among the bishops, which is an internal ontological unity analogous to the *communio* that makes all baptized into one body. It is a *communio* within a *communio*. This unity is the foundation for external collegial structures and practices. The theory (surely well within Christian tradition) has an intrinsic coherence; it is in harmony with historical data and attractive in its simplicity and clarity. It certainly provides good material for a vigorous debate.

Joseph Cardinal Ratzinger, now Pope Benedict XVI, initiated such a debate—without himself explicitly taking a position in it. After I published a brief commentary on *Apostolos suos* (of which the above chapter is a revised and enlarged edition) in *Stimmen der Zeit,*[15] the then Prefect of the Congregation for the Doctrine of Faith requested the editor of the journal to publish a response by Winfried Aymans, professor of canon law at the University of Munich.[16] Professor Aymans' answer, however, remained within the framework of the recent canonical ordinances without reflecting on the common tradition of the Eastern and Western churches, and without engaging in the debate on

---

15. "Die Bishofskonferenzen und die Macht des Geistes," *Stimmen der Zeit* 218 (2000) 3–18.

16. "Geistlose Bischofskonferenzen?" ibid., 408–19; my response, "Anmerkungen," ibid., 419–22.

a historical and theological level. In his piece, an example of canonical positivism, neither East and West nor theology and canon law have met.

The church would benefit from a thorough critical discussion about and around this issue. In truth, we had little, if any, debate among the bishops (let alone among the theologians) before *Apostolos suos* was promulgated, although the *sensus fidei* of the bishops' *communio* has its irreplaceable role in the process. Future exchanges, however, must not remain on a purely abstract level; they should take into account the practical implications and consequences of the differing theories. For instance, if there is truth in the theory that the bishops and their legitimate gatherings represent a divinely willed "principle of diversity" in the church, then in the appointments of bishops, candidates with a creative mind and a capacity to take initiatives need to be favored. If unity must be the paramount consideration, candidates who excel in the virtue of loyalty and obedience should be selected.

We have at hand an issue to show (and to warn) us that a seemingly subtle and abstract theological position in the first place can shape the face of the church in the practical order for centuries to come. It can have an immense impact on the daily life of the faithful, on the internal life of the community, and beyond those, on the ecumenical movement and the evangelization of the nations. We can only gain by intelligent and grace-filled debates.

3

Discourse about the Laity
A Sacred Power

Today, one of the most debated issues in the church concerns the laity. Questions are raised far and wide: Who are the laity? What is their role? Or: In the best state of the church, what would be the rights and duties of the laity?

In searching for the correct response, I initially followed the traditional path set by practical theologians and reflective canon lawyers:[1] I took the sharp distinction between the laity and the hierarchy for granted and was ready to sketch a "theology of the laity." But gradually I became aware that I was trying to respond to a faulty question that can lead only to a deficient conclusion. The laity—set apart—cannot be the subject of a self-contained and adequate theological or canonical treatise because the laity does not exist in that manner. It is no more an autonomous part of the social body of the church than the heart is an autonomous organ in a living human body.

The laity in its entirety and the hierarchy together constitute the people of God. Together they are the one social body of the church that is internally structured in a unique manner. No self-standing "theology" of one part can be construed; no norms for the operation of the one can be set without taking into account the task of the other. The laity comes to life and best operates when it is harmoniously blended with the hierarchy. The hierarchy simply cannot exist without the laity. They are meant to support and balance each other. They exist and work for a common purpose.

THE PRESENT STATE OF THE LAITY

In the beginning of this twenty-first century we live in the middle of a paradox—and the faithful are hardly aware of it. On the one hand, the pronouncements of Vatican Council II brought remarkable results and opened the door

---

1. For example, Yves Congar, *Lay People in the Church: A Study for a Theology of Laity* (London: Geoffrey Chapman, 1965); Gustave Thils, *Les laïcs dans le nouveau Code de droit canonique et au IIe Concile du Vatican* (Louvain-la Neuve: Faculté de Théologie, 1983).

for an increased promotion of the laity. On the other hand, the official policy of the church based on a recent theological opinion that found its way into the revised Code of Canon Law excludes the laity from any *major* decision-making processes—reversing an immemorial tradition. We live in a time of progress and regress.

INTRODUCTION TO THE PROBLEM: A POPE'S LAST TESTAMENT

The following is an excerpt from the memoirs of Alex Carter (1909–2002), former Bishop of Sault Ste. Marie, Ontario, Canada.[2] Carter describes a farewell talk by Pope Pius XI to a group of Canadian students—he was one of them. It was a farewell talk in more than one sense. The students were returning home, and the pope knew his days on earth were numbered. The bishop recalls:

> Our most striking meeting with [Pius XI] took place [in 1939] at a special audi-
> ence held during the 50th anniversary celebrations of the Canadian College,
> led by Monseigneur Perrin. He was visibly weakened. Every now and then, [his]
> eyes would flash and a little of his old vigour would come back, but this strong
> man, who had been an Alpine climber and who usually looked so powerful, was
> obviously in physical pain. He would slump a little in his chair and then pull
> himself up again as he gave us a most striking talk. It was not very long, but it
> was very prophetic. He said something like this:
>
>> "You are the young priests who have come to Rome. You are going back
>> to Canada and will continue to build the Church there. I do not place any
>> limits on the providence of God, but I am sure that my life expectancy is
>> very short. I want you to take this message away with you. The Church,
>> the mystical Body of Christ, has become a monstrosity. The head is very
>> large, but the body is shrunken. You, the priests, must rebuild that body
>> of the Church and the only way that you can rebuild it is to mobilize the
>> lay people. You must call upon the lay people to become, along with you,
>> the witnesses of Christ. You must call them especially to bring Christ
>> back to the workplace, to the marketplace."
>
> This powerful message was like a Last Will and Testament of the Pope. As a matter
> of fact that was his last public audience. All audiences were cancelled the following
> day and he died not long afterwards. From the beginning of his Pontificate, Pius
> XI was the Pope of Catholic Action. He was the one who had often written to the

---

2. Carter was ordained priest for the Diocese of Montreal. He studied canon law at St. Apollinaris in Rome and was resident of the Canadian College. He became coadjutor Bishop of Sault Ste. Marie in 1956, was consecrated in 1957, and succeeded to the See in 1958. He attended all the sessions of Vatican Council II, was president of the Canadian Conference of Bishops from 1967–1969 and its elected delegate at the synod of Bishops in 1969 and 1971. On having reached the statutory age limit, he resigned his See in 1985.

Bishops of the world, calling for the participation of lay people in the work of evangelization. Thus it was in keeping with his own teaching that he gave us this last message—a message from the grave, you could almost say. The memory of the moment remains with me. I can visualize it, even now, in my old age. I have never forgotten that audience and as a matter of fact, I believe that it has shaped, in part, my own life and my approach to my role as pastor, chaplain, and bishop.[3]

ANALYSIS OF THE POPE'S DIAGNOSIS: A NEW TYPE OF CRISIS

Referring to the church, the pope speaks of a "monster," not a flattering image, certainly not from the lips of a pope. What is he suggesting?

By "monster," he presumably means a living and functioning organism that is ill structured and dysfunctional. He tries to convey a hard truth through a dramatic word: he sees the church as suffering from a lack of structural balance and of some dislocation in its vital operations. "The head is very large but the body is shrunken"—one organ has grown beyond its due size and is encroaching on the others. By saying that "the head is very large," he can mean only that the hierarchy has overreached its normal limits, has grown weightier than is good for the rest of the people, and its overwhelming presence impedes the normal functioning of the rest. By speaking of "the shrunken body," he can refer only to the laity that is underdeveloped and deprived of the use of its potential.

The crisis is of internal origin. An external enemy has not brought it on. The vital balances that govern the body and keep it sound are out of order. The affliction impedes the normal working of energies hidden in the "shrunken members." Inevitably, some external consequences follow: the attractive beauty of the community is lost precisely because beauty exists in the right balances.[4]

This is the state of the church seen by Pope Pius XI, in 1938, at the end of his life. After Vatican Council II, does his judgment still stand?

AFTER VATICAN COUNCIL II:
EXPANSION OF THE ROLE OF THE LAITY

Vatican Council II, in its great charter, the Dogmatic Constitution on the Church (*Lumen gentium*), repeatedly affirmed the dignity of the universal "people of God"—to which the laity belong. Within the same Constitution, the Council dedicated an entire chapter to explaining the doctrinal foundation

---

3. Alex Carter, *A Canadian Bishop's Memoirs* (North Bay, Ontario: Tomiko Publications, 1994) 50–51.

4. The consequences are bound to be far reaching: a community whose image is not attractive is not likely to expand. Go and preach to all nations: grow and show God's beauty. Beauty is harmony of proportions.

of the laity's position and vocation. Further, in its Decree on the Apostolate of the Laity (*Apostolicam actuositatem,* a document more practically oriented), the Council acknowledged the right of the laity to proclaim the Good News and to witness for Christ on the strength of their baptism, without any need "to be mandated by the hierarchy."

As a result, after the Council, laypersons emerged as ministers of the Gospel in a great variety of situations. Today we see them having a visible role in liturgical celebrations, occupying diocesan offices, directing Catholic educational and charitable works, voicing their concerns in councils and synods, and so forth.

For such progress, we must rejoice.

AFTER VATICAN COUNCIL II: RESTRICTION OF THE ROLE OF THE LAITY

After the Council, however, a new provision in canon law moved in the opposite direction. It excluded laypersons from significant decision-making processes where ecclesiastical "jurisdiction" is in play. The provision is now honored in practice: no layperson is a member, or for that matter a "major official" (a technical term, well defined in law) of a Roman congregation; no layperson has a vote within synods and councils of higher rank (although they may be present in a lesser capacity); no lay judge at an ecclesiastical court may function as a single judge.[5] In sum, no layperson is admitted "into the inner sanctuary" that is to have a significant role in building the church from within.[6]

Let the Code of Canon Law speak:

> Canon 129 § 1—Those who have received sacred orders are qualified, according to the norm of the prescripts of the law, for the power of governance, which exists in the church by divine institution and is also called the power of jurisdiction.
>
> § 2—Lay members of the Christian faithful can cooperate in the exercise of this same power according to the norm of the law.

The two paragraphs taken together state and rule that

* they who have received sacred orders have the capacity to exercise the "power of governance,"
* this power is of divine institution,
* this power is identical with the power traditionally known as "jurisdiction,"

---

5. See Canon 1421 § 2.

6. The difference between an "advisor" and a "participant in a dialogue" is that the former is outside the creative process of the giving and taking of an exchange, the latter is inside it.

* no layperson is capable of exercising this power,
* laypersons can cooperate with the ordained without participating in the power.

Such a neat and radical exclusion of the laity from any participation in the power of governance is discontinuous with an immemorial tradition. It is an innovation. The opinion that inspired it is not "what has everywhere, always, by all, been believed" (*quod ubique, quod semper, quod ab omnibus creditum est*)—to use the well-known criteria of Vincent of Lerrin.

Recalling a few historical facts, events, and structures that *were in the past recognized as legitimate* should be enough to show that the new rule is a break with the Tradition and that laypersons did indeed *participate* in the power of governance.

The ecumenical councils of the first millennium, called by the Byzantine emperors and empresses, were surely acts of jurisdiction by laymen and laywomen. The majority of the participants at the Council of Florence were not "in orders"; therefore, "lay votes" had a real impact on the determinations concerning the reunion of the Eastern and Western churches. Abbesses for centuries exercised "quasi-episcopal jurisdiction" in governing "quasi-dioceses"—except in dispensing the sacraments, for which ordination was necessary. Such lay "prelates" had the "power of jurisdiction"—with the full and direct support of the Holy See well into the nineteenth century.[7]

History is not on the side of Canon 129. Therefore, the restriction can hardly be grounded in dogma. It must be a disciplinary provision, and if so, it can be changed. Participation of the laity in the power of governance cannot be absolutely excluded, but it must be integrated into the higher power conferred on the hierarchy by the sacrament of orders.[8]

If Canon 129 has no roots in the past, whence does it come?

THE THEORY OF "*THE* SACRED POWER"

With Canon 129 comes a newly intuited understanding of the episcopal power that was given a new name: "*the* sacred power."[9] When the expression

---

7. For more explanation and documentation see Ladislas Orsy, "Lay Persons in Church Governance: A Disputed Question," *America* 174 (1996) 10–13.

8. For a concise exegesis of Canon 129, see *Il Codice di Diritto Canonico* by Luigi Chiappetta, vol. 1 (Rome: Dehoniane, 1996) 202–5. He gives a concise, clear, and fairly comprehensive survey of the legal issues. What he says, however, needs to be completed and corrected by taking into consideration the historical sources and the relevant theological values.

9. See Adriano Celeghin, *Origine e natura della potestà sacra: Posizioni postconciliari* (Brescia: Morcelliana, 1987).

was introduced into the theological and canonical literature in the postconciliar years, it was new, but by now it has become standard. It is the specific sacramental gift (charism) conferred by episcopal ordination. When broadly interpreted, it includes the combined powers to teach (prophet), to sanctify (priest), and to govern (king); when used strictly, it refers exclusively to the power of governance, *potestas regendi* or *regiminis*, called also "jurisdiction," as in Canon 129.

This new theory should have begun its life among theologians at the stage of a "disputed question" and it should have gone through a crucible of their critical assessment *before it reached the state of standard language.* This did not happen, certainly not to a sufficient degree. Now through policies and laws, it shapes the future of the church. Theologians (who could evaluate it in function of the sources) have scarcely taken notice of the new language, let alone the doctrine behind it. Canon lawyers whose primary interest is in practicalities simply take the new approach for granted.

Some reservation, however, should be voiced.

* To appropriate the expression "*the* sacred power" exclusively for the episcopal power shows a lack of good manners in theology and an unnecessary rhetoric in canon law. "*The* sacred power" in (of) the church is vested in the entire people of God through the all-pervading presence of the Spirit. It is present and operative in the ordained and non-ordained; for this the people *unfailingly adhere to the faith, penetrate it more deeply through right judgment, and apply it in daily life* (cf. LG 12). Episcopal power is privileged participation in the power of the Spirit.[10]

* The doctrine that non-ordained persons can only cooperate with the power of governance but not participate in it assumes that the said power is indivisible. This is surely incorrect because whatever power a bishop has, it comes from two sources, the human and the divine. The church, before being a grace-filled assembly, is a human community that demands a functioning order to exist. There is no theological reason why a bishop could not let a qualified person "participate" in his power to govern provided such participation does not encroach on the exclusive charism that is given by ordination.

* As it is, the doctrine perpetuates and supports a sharp separation between the laity and the hierarchy.[11]

---

10. The wedding liturgy of the Eastern church brings out clearly that the sacrament of matrimony confers a sacred power on the spouses to generate and educate children.

11. No better example could be found to show how one single word in the law can give a new direction to the life of the church for centuries to come and have an impact on the worldwide operation of the community as well as on the life of the individuals in local parishes.

A LINGUISTIC SHIFT AND A STRUCTURAL CHANGE

The first Code of Canon Law promulgated in 1917 stated in Canon 118: "Clerics only can (*possunt*, 'are able') obtain (*obtinere*, 'to receive and to possess') the power of orders and of jurisdiction."

The same Code defined clerics in Canon 108 as "they who have been installed (*mancipati*) by first tonsure in divine ministries."[12]

The second Code of Canon Law promulgated in 1983 states in Canon 207 § 1: "By divine institution, there are among the Christian faithful in the Church sacred ministers who in law are also called clerics; the other members of the Christian faithful are called lay persons."

Further, Canon 266 § 1 states: "Through the reception of the diaconate, a person becomes a cleric . . ."[13]

And Canon 274 § 1 adds: "Only clerics can obtain offices for whose exercise the power of orders or the power of ecclesiastical governance is required."

As the quotes show, behind the linguistic shift a real change has occurred in the definition of a "cleric." Until 1972 tonsure, not ordination, made a cleric. In the new regime ordination to the diaconate does it. Tonsure was a purely ritual act, not a sacrament; the theological status of the tonsured person remained exactly what it was. He continued to be a layperson. Yet from the moment he received the tonsure he could participate (and many did) in the exercise of the power of governance, *in potestate regiminis*, which is now the exclusive domain of the ordained persons.

The linguistic change, however, left the door open to a substantial doctrinal misunderstanding. Some may claim that nothing has changed: clerics and clerics only can participate in the power to govern. The contention is correct—if nothing matters but language. Otherwise we have a structural change: the laity has been excluded from participation.

If the present situation becomes a norm for the future, the church will be more clerical than it ever was. Since the laity will have no part in any major decision-making office or process, much of their God-given gifts and talents will lay fallow. The hierarchy will stress to them that obedience ought to be

---

I am thinking of the word *cooperari*, "to cooperate," in Canon 129 § 2. It shows also the singular priority that laws can have in the existential order.

12. Tonsure is a religious ceremony, a partial cutting of the hair or some shaving of the head. It is of monastic origin, but from the sixth century it developed into *the* sign of admission to the clerical state. It was never considered part of the sacrament of orders. In 1972 Paul VI abolished it and declared that the entry into the clerical state is the ordination to the diaconate. See MP *Ministeria quaedam*, AAS 64 (1972) 529–34.

13. See also Canon 1008.

their principal virtue. Sure, the laity will be promoted in many minor ways, but the line between the ordained and non-ordained will remain sharply drawn.

In particular, no woman will ever have the opportunity (or capacity) to have a share in major decision-making processes—not even when the subject matter of a decision does not require the sacramental power of ordination.

We need to think afresh.

LET US RETURN TO THE ORIGINAL QUESTION:
WHO ARE THE LAITY?

Whenever I am invited to speak on "The Theology of the Laity," I never argue about the title. But once there (say, at the parish), by way of introducing my subject, I ask the laypeople, *"At what point in your life did you become a layperson?"* As a rule, they look surprised. Then, after some hesitation, they say, "at baptism."

"Yes, but," I continue, "were you baptized to be 'laypersons' forever?"

In response, a consensus soon emerges that all of us, laity and clerics, were baptized to be God's people—with all the gifts that such an exalted status implies. Baptism brings a substantial equality to all and it is never to be lost. To speak at that point of the "special charism of the laity" does not make sense.[14]

All this leads to a theological starting point that no sacrament, sacramental, or institutional rite in the church would (could) confer "the charism of laity"—as sacraments do confer a specific charism.[15]

Continuing my conversation with the audience, to consolidate this conclusion, I press further, *"How do you define the laity?"*

The response is mostly prompt and clear: they are the non-ordained.

"Yes, but," I retort, "can something that exists be defined by a negative sentence that simply states the absence of a substance—such as that of priesthood?"

Obviously, not. It follows that we cannot construe a theology, let alone a rich theology, of the "charism of the laity" when there is no evidence of any particular sacramental (or lesser) action that would confer such specific

14. This is not to say that the Spirit could not, or would not, or does not ever grant a special charism "to sanctify the world," that is, to sanctify some aspect of the secular world, but it is to say that such charism—when granted—is not the specific fruit of any sacrament or any sacramental.

It would be wrong to assume that a charism seemingly for the sanctification of the "secular" follows the status of a person in the church; history shows a much broader picture. Gregory the Great (a cleric) certainly did much for the betterment of the secular state of the city of Rome, and Catherine of Siena (a laic) worked powerfully for the internal health of the church.

15. In scholastic language *ex opere operato*, an expression much maligned but that retains a sound meaning even outside the "School": a sacrament is a gesture of Christ that confers grace—precisely because a gesture of Christ cannot be grace-less—assuming the recipient is disposed to receive the gift.

charism. Nor can the nature of this charism be explained by a purely negative affirmation with no positive content.

But we have by no means come to a dead end. We are learning a lesson that in order to understand the place and the role of the laity in the church, we must not look at the laity as a distinct unit in the church. We must focus on the entire people as a whole. When we contemplate the undivided body and watch its organic and harmonious operation, we are in position to assess the place and role of its parts.

Vatican Council II gives us an authentic description of God's people and of their gifts:

> The holy people of God share also in Christ's prophetic office: it spreads abroad a living witness to him, especially by a life of faith and love and by offering to God a sacrifice of praise, the fruit of lips confessing his name. . . . The whole body of the faithful who have received an anointing which comes from the holy one . . . cannot fail in belief (*in credendo falli nequit*). It shows this characteristic through the entire people's supernatural sense of the faith, when "from the bishops to the last of the faithful" it manifests a universal consensus in matters of faith and morals. By this sense of faith, aroused and sustained by the Spirit of truth, the people of God, guided by the sacred magisterium which it faithfully obeys, receives not the word of human beings, but truly the word of God . . . "the faith once delivered to the saints." . . . The people unfailingly adheres (*indefectibiliter adhaeret*) to this faith, penetrates it more deeply through right judgment, and applies it more fully to daily life. (LG 12)

The Council names two principal gifts that God has granted, and continues to grant, directly to his people baptized with living faith, hope, and love: infallibility in belief and indefectibility in right judgment.

In other words, God has entrusted the history of salvation, the subject of our belief, to the memory of the entire people. God has endowed the church with the prudence that is necessary in daily life to reach salvation. Some portion of that infallibility and indefectibility belongs to the non-ordained—otherwise it cannot belong to the "whole." Divine light and divine energy is diffused in the whole church. How can the right balance in the body of the church be restored?[16]

THE ROLE OF THE HIERARCHY

It should be enough to recall what we hold for our faith.

---

16. When the church appears to be in ferment and even in confusion, we should be slow to blame the people. The root of the trouble may well be that there is a lot of holy but unused energy around, precisely in the people—in women as well as men—with no outlet. It is the nature of energy, any energy, to become restless when it is compelled to be idle. When it is given scope, it can produce fruit hundredfold.

The episcopal college, with the bishop of Rome presiding over it, is assisted by the Spirit to proclaim the evangelical message and to be the ultimate judge in doctrinal matters. The bishops, and in a special way the bishop of Rome, are the authentic witnesses of our Tradition, but the history of God's self-revelation and mighty deeds lives in the memory of all the people. Further, the episcopal college as a corporation and the individual bishops in their dioceses are mandated "in the Spirit" to bring and sustain "tranquility in order" so that the communities may live in peace and the church may prosper, but the practical prudence needed for fair and balanced judgments is spread among all the members.

Thus, nothing is taken away from the traditional role of the hierarchy. But their role is defined with greater precision. The Spirit assists them, but they emerge from among the people; they must turn to the entire people for the full memory of the evangelical message; they need the prudent help of the people in practical matters. In so many ways, the hierarchy depends on the people, and of course, it exists for the well-being of all.

THE FUTURE

A trend that has affected the church for centuries cannot be changed overnight. But the work for change may start right now. First and foremost, the minds and hearts of all the people ought to be lifted up to a higher viewpoint where they begin to discover and appreciate the riches of God's gift in the entire body. The hierarchy need to affirm their mandate but must also proclaim the riches of the rest—and the limits of their own charism. The so-called laity should come to a better knowledge and a stronger awareness of what they possess and how much they can contribute to the building of the church; they are God's people. Without such conversion, little can be done.

Then the legal barrier contained in Canon 129 that allows the non-clerics to cooperate only with the "power of governance" but not to participate in any way must be removed. Once done, the search for new balances can take off. The search itself should be both theoretical and practical. The theoretical inquiry must proceed in the usual manner of theological quests, moving from the data of revelation through creative but well-grounded insights to firm proposals. The practical search should rely on the sense of faith and religious prudence by shifting responsibilities from the hierarchy to the rest of the faithful so as to restore the shrunken members to their pristine strength, and relieve the head of unnecessary burden. A delicate operation—in a sensitive body![17]

---

17. Here is an attempt to make some practical suggestions. They may look simple and small, but, in truth, they are like the mustard seed: they contain a potential that can bring a growth that all will admire.

PAUL THE APOSTLE SPEAKS

Around the year A.D. 52 Paul wrote his first letter to the Corinthians. Interestingly, he addressed it not to any leader but "to the church of God which is at Corinth, to those sanctified in Christ Jesus, called to be saints . . ." (1 Cor 1:2). He then states: "To each is given the manifestation of the Spirit for the common good. To one is given through the Spirit the utterance of wisdom, and to another the utterance of knowledge according to the same Spirit . . ." (12:7-8). Paul goes on to enumerate the various gifts of the Spirit manifested in the community: the gift of healing, the working of miracles, prophecy, discernment of spirits, various kinds of tongues, and the interpretation of tongues. He tells them to bring order to their meetings, but he is equally emphatic that they should not extinguish the Spirit.

If Paul the Apostle ever returned to the face of the earth and found a church where silent obedience is the rule far and wide, a church without the merry manifestations of the gifts of the Spirit, one wonders: what would Paul say?[18]

Our tradition admits the participation of laypersons in decision-making processes, which are an integral part of the governance of the church. Granted, the unique character of the episcopal power ought to be respected, but the power given through baptism must not be frustrated. To work out the formalities and the details, creative theologians and canon lawyers are needed. They could start their work immediately.

Laypersons could be voting members of synods or councils. (Some earlier ecumenical councils permitted it; surely, it was not a doctrinal deviation.) There is no theological reason why persons without orders could not be members of some decision-making bodies in the ordinary administration of the church, e.g., some of the Roman congregations and offices. (Often one hears the suggestion that laypersons should be made cardinals in order to participate in such tasks. That is hardly a good idea because it demeans the dignity that baptism confers. They should be invited for what they are: people of God.)

Laypersons could be in charge of the administration of the assets of the church. Those duly qualified could be officially designated as the preachers of the Word.

The basis for such commission should be *the sacred power* given to every Christian through baptism. Then, in this way, we honor the mystery and let faith seek not only understanding but also practical action.

18. Many Christian women may sigh and say: Was it not Paul who wrote that ". . . the women should keep silence in the churches. . ." (1 Cor 14:34)? How can we expect him to stand up for us? The correct answer may well be that Paul (like Peter) had his weak moments; he too was a fragile person. After all, on a deeper doctrinal level, he wrote that in the church ". . . there is neither male nor female; for you are all one in Christ Jesus" (Gal 3:28). Paul failed in adjusting his practical advice to the doctrine he preached, as Peter failed to live up to received teaching in Antioch when he refused to eat with the Gentiles. Paul responded forcefully and corrected him. In the history of the church women such as Catherine of Siena, Teresa of Avila (now doctors of the church), even more, countless women who handed down the faith through teaching succeeding generations have responded forcefully to Paul and corrected him. Looking at these women, what would Paul say? Probably, certainly, "I stand corrected."

4

Toward the One Church of Christ
Has Ecumenism a Future?

O n November 21, 1964, after much argument and with great rejoicing, the bishops assembled at Vatican Council II solemnly approved the Decree on Ecumenism. Ever since then we pause, time after time, and ponder as we assess our progress toward the one and only church of Christ. How far have we come? How much remains to be done?

The recounting of some recent facts and events may very well cause a somber mood: the progress is slow and much remains to be done. The goal, the blessed unity of all Christians, appears as elusive as ever—if not more so. We are tempted to say with a heavy heart, like the two disciples on the road to Emmaus, "But we had hoped that he was the one to redeem Israel . . ." (Luke 24:21).

Here are some findings that can hardly be contested:

* The dialogues increasingly reveal their limits. As appointed groups of experts meet each other, they succeed in creating friendly relationships. They raise pertinent questions and listen to learned answers. They apologize for past wrongs, and they reach a consensus time and again on a (subtle) point of doctrine. Yet no matter how much they may accomplish, they leave more undone. Judging by what they have achieved over some forty years, by any reasonable estimate centuries more of conversations are needed to reach the communion of minds and hearts that Christ prayed for.

* While the experts are doing their selfless work, large segments of ordinary Christian people of different denominations remain content to be as they are and feel no pressing need for a greater unity. Bad memories may hamper them, or unconsciously absorbed prejudices may hold them back. Yet committees of specialists cannot achieve full communion: a mass movement of the faithful alone can bring it about. The one and only church of Christ cannot exist without the people (saints

and sinners) from all corners of the earth crowding into it—all *being of one heart and soul* (see Acts 4:32). The lesson of the aftermath of the Council of Florence (1439–1445) must not be forgotten. Although at the Council the representatives of the Eastern church consented to the union, when they returned home with the agreement, the people rejected it. And that was the end of the reconciliation.

* In spite of the expanded efforts for union, new disagreements are emerging in various communities. The Episcopalian (Anglican) Church is struggling with centrifugal forces. The autonomous churches of the East are searching, through many difficulties, for the correct relationships among themselves. There is disunity among the Lutheran synods. Behind the present apparent calm in the Roman Catholic communion, strong conflicting dynamics are testing the strength of unifying forces.

* Reliable witnesses, be they detached observers or engaged workers, keep reporting signs of tiredness, indifference, even despair in the cause of unity. Admittedly, it may be difficult to prove such hearsay by hard evidence; but the witnesses are too numerous and their voices too strong to be ignored.

Facts and events do not lie. On no account should we deny them or cover them up with an irrational rhetoric of optimism. No serious thinking or effective work can be done in God's kingdom without the utmost respect for verifiable facts and occurring events: God is in the real.

But if God is in the real, we should take a second look at the whole extent of "the real." God's plan is broader than what our senses can perceive. Hence the questions: Is our interpretation of the facts and events correct? Have we grasped their *full* meaning? Remember how the two disciples left Jerusalem and took the road to Emmaus because, as they were told by the Stranger who joined them, they failed to understand the Scriptures. Are we like them? Do we say, "We had hoped," and walk away from God's plan because we do not understand the grace-filled time of God? Could it be that God's plan is unfolding precisely through the facts and events narrated, but we are not reading God's plan correctly?

What follows is an attempt to penetrate into the deeper meaning, the mystery, of the ecumenical movement within the horizon of faith, hope, and love—the only way we can enter into God's plan. My intent is not to deny or to cover up sobering facts and events; it is to discover how they are part of a greater project. If there is a way of overcoming the crisis, it is not in trying to change occurrences over which we have no power but in changing our attitudes toward handling them.

THE ONE CHURCH OF CHRIST IN FOCUS

The Goal and Measure of Ecumenical Efforts

The ecumenical movement makes sense because we believe that the one and only church of Christ exists in God's plan. Christ prayed for it on the solemn night of his *transitus*: his prayer could not have been in vain. Hence, our duty is to build this church, even if as of yet we have had no glimpse of its internal harmony in unity and diversity, even if we have not seen its glory.

When Vatican Council II declared that the church of Christ subsists in the Roman Catholic Church, the Council meant that we are in possession of the fullness of revelation; but in no way did the Council affirm that we understand what we have in all its breadth and depth. Hence we can believe in both the present fullness and the future revelation of riches.

Further, in our theological imagination we should never see this future church of Christ as merely a religious phenomenon isolated from the rest of human history. It is God's gift to the whole human family: the very threshold of salvation for all generations to come. St. Paul writes, "for the creation waits with eager longing for the revealing of the children of God" (Rom 8:19), and "the whole creation has been groaning in travail together until now" (Rom 8:22). In a mysterious way, the one church of Christ is instrumental in the redemption and exaltation of the whole creation.

When we position the future church of Christ as the goal and measure of the ecumenical movement, the very nature of the movement reveals itself with a clarity and simplicity that otherwise we cannot have. Ultimately, the goal of the movement is not to reach mutual agreements among the churches but for each community to transform itself into the image of the one church of Christ—as far as they can discern it. The ecumenical task consists of a continuous effort to know the mystery better and to move toward it. Then, agreements among the separated communities are bound to follow.

The dialogues should be seen as forms of mutual assistance among believing people to help each other to penetrate the Word of God to a greater depth. *There*, they will find unity; *there*, they will cease to disagree.

The ecumenical dialogues should be common efforts to receive the gift of unity from God. We are disposed to receive this gift through the theological virtues of faith, hope, and love.

In the Light of Faith

Faith reveals that: (1) the Spirit of God alone has the power to create or restore the one church of Christ, and the divine Spirit, the Creator, alone can give us the vision and energy to build it; (2) such work of the Spirit is discernable in recent developments; (3) in fact, the Spirit has already created a substantial unity among the Christian people.

First, *we believe in the authority of our Tradition, reaffirmed by Vatican Council II, that only the Spirit, the Creator, has the power to establish the one and only church of Christ.* The conciliar texts amount to a profession of faith:

> It is the Holy Spirit, dwelling in those who believe and pervading and ruling over the entire church, who brings about that wonderful communion of the faithful and joins them together so intimately in Christ that he is the principle of the church's unity. (UR, Decree on Ecumenism, 2)

> Further, this council declares that it realizes that this holy objective—the reconciliation of all Christians in the unity of the one and only church of Christ—transcends human powers and gifts. (Ibid. 24)

The Council says with no ambiguity that the Holy Spirit is the originator of the movement for union and communion, and the Spirit remains in charge of it. We humans can be cooperators but not creators. For this course we cannot lay down our own laws and conditions.

Second, *the history of the postconciliar years offers quasi-empirical evidence that the Holy Spirit is indeed in charge and active.* All we need is to put side by side what happened (or did not happen) in the four centuries after the Council of Trent and what we can observe in recent decades. Attitudes of extreme rigidity that pervaded generations of people and communities have literally melted away—if not everywhere, certainly far and wide—and have given place to a disposition of openness and flexibility. Christians who once refused even to say an Our Father together learned to praise the Lord with one voice—even if they have not come so far as to share the eucharistic table. We must admit that such deep transformation of attitudes could not have happened without an immensely strong injection of healing grace, originating from the Holy Spirit, into the communities.

Third, *we know that through our faith a substantial unity already exists among the Christian communities.* Admittedly, the language we use daily misleads us into thinking otherwise. We speak of "our separated brothers and sisters." But the fundamental truth is that through our common baptism and profession that "Jesus is Lord" (1 Cor 12:3), our brothers and sisters not of the Roman communion are united to us as we are united to them.

Ordinarily, the fact of historical separation dominates our discourse. Yet the ontological reality (what is actually real) is that the Spirit, in whom we dwell and who dwells in us, holds all baptized believers together. It makes a difference if the ecumenical movement consists in working for the reconciliation of separated bodies, or if it is a healing process within one sacramental but internally wounded body. In the former case, negotiations take primary importance. In the latter case, the real work consists in removing external impediments and giving full scope to the internal forces present in the entire body.

Hope Divine

The theological virtue of hope is often misunderstood: we conceive it on the pattern of human hope. On an earthly level, "to hope" is to define expectations (variously grounded) for the future, and then cling to them—no matter what may happen. Obviously, to hope in this manner may lead to a disregard of facts and events and to a stubborn pursuit of a fallacy that can lead only to disaster.

Divine hope is radically different: it looks more at the present than at the future. It leads to surrender to God who is in charge of events. It blends into God's plan—here and now. It creates an unbounded and well-grounded optimism in the one who hopes. God guarantees a good outcome but without telling us what it will be. Divine hope positions a human person into the flow of God's project; the human person joins in God's creative activity.

In this prospect the sobering and depressing facts and events reveal their true nature: they are part of God's plan, a plan of which we see only some fragments. Considered in isolation from their broader context, they may be disappointing, but as parts of a whole, they are bound to make sense.

A comparison comes to mind. Imagine a medieval architect who is asked to design and build a cathedral with all its magnificence: the soaring towers, the flying buttresses, the rose windows—also the impish gargoyles on the roof. He, the architect, sees the entire project, but then, sensibly, he portions out the work among his apprentices. They will be in charge of the parts assigned to them, and some of them will do no more than design and build the ugly shapes of the gargoyles. God has designed his own cathedral. We are the apprentices—at times assigned to attend only to the gargoyles.

The theological foundation for this understanding of the virtue of hope is in the Scriptures. When Mary of Nazareth pronounced, "let it be to me according to your word" (Luke 1:38), she signaled that she was willing to surrender herself to a plan that she did not know or certainly could not direct in any way. As she found out later, the plan was full of somber facts and events. Her participation in God's project was perfect. She never said, "I had hoped."

We have reached a point where the assessment of the ecumenical movement in function of faith, hope, and love reveals its internal cohesiveness and essential soundness. Faith brings an intelligence that no human insight could give. Hope opens the door to enter and blend into the dynamics of a divine plan. Love leads to action that no human strength could sustain.

Magnanimity as Love Divine

Love consists not in words but in deeds. Christ repeatedly stated it, saints practiced it, sages affirmed it, and doctors tried to explain it.

Love in God, then, is synonymous with giving, but this inclination to give is not a mere attribute. When God spoke to Moses from the midst of a burning bush, Moses asked, "If I come to the people of Israel . . . and they ask me, 'What is his name?' what shall I say to them?" God responded, "I am who I am" (Exod 3:13-14). God could have said, "*I am who gives*"; that is, "*I am Goodness effusive.*" God's very nature is to communicate himself. Within God and inwardly, there is circumincession, *perichoresis*, the interpenetration of the three Persons; true communication although beyond our intelligence. Within God but outwardly, there is the effusion of life—the act of creation—that brings us existence and sustenance.

Let us call this divine giving "magnanimity"—a word borrowed from the philosophy of Aristotle where it has a finite meaning, but a word that can be stretched to reach into the infinite. Magnanimity is divine when it means to give from an inexhaustible internal resource without expecting any reward, because God is the inexhaustible internal resource.

Such love must be the operating principle of the ecumenical movement. Its source is the living Spirit that all communities possess through their baptism and their gift of faith. It follows that their prime concern should not be *What could we do?* but *How can we remove the impediments surging from our narrow humanity and let the dynamics of the Spirit prevail?*

The acceptance of the vision of faith and the surrender in hope leads to the operation of love, a divine manner of life. But how do we apply this theory? Without finding a way of practicing it in our daily work for unity, beautiful as our words may be, they are no more than the sounds of "a noisy gong or a clanging cymbal" (1 Cor 13:1).

In recent years, two practical proposals emerged for effectively promoting the cause of unity among Christian churches (no matter what the observers may report). Both are demanding and both demand the communities to give, perhaps in a somewhat metaphorical sense, but still to give. Both ask for giving in a divine manner, that is, from the internal resources of each community and without expectation of reward. Both are radical requests for down-to-earth manifestations of magnanimity.

Above all, both are immediately feasible.

One is *the way of kenosis*, proposed by the Groupe des Dombes in France; the other is *the way of learning and receiving*, suggested by the participants of the Durham Colloquium in January 2006. The former speaks of giving up, or giving away what hampers unity; the latter speaks of giving space to the gifts of grace and wisdom coming from others.

The way of kenosis was suggested first by the Groupe des Dombes, a permanent association of ecumenists founded by Paul Couturier in 1937 that meets yet today. Their method of seeking ecumenical understanding through intense periods of prayer and the reading of early Christian sources could serve as a model for all.

Their proposal is grounded in the analysis of the identity of Christian churches. They see it as composed of three elements. In its core, each communion has a substantial Christian identity, which is not negotiable. Then, in the course of history, each developed a unique "personality," for example, Orthodox, Roman, Lutheran, and so forth, which should not be abandoned since it may represent due diversity. Finally, each denomination has confessional characteristics, accretions by historical accidents, devotional customs, and ritual observances, all of which are not indispensable and—to some and varying degrees—could be sacrificed for the sake of unity.

The ecumenical task for each church is then to turn inward and ask: What is in our manner of life that does not belong to the Christian core? What is not part of the beauty of our unique personality? Which among our unnecessary heirlooms could be sacrificed for the sake of unity?

Releasing precious possessions to enter a world of poverty can be the correct path toward unity. This is how Christ enriched the world: "though he was in the form of God, he did not count equality with God a thing to be grasped, but emptied [*ekenosen*] himself" (Phil 2:5-6). This is how individual communities can build the one church of Christ.

A potential misunderstanding should be discarded: in no way does the Groupe des Dombes suggest that the exercise of kenosis should ever allow anyone to abandon the truth for some comfortable common denominator. The way of kenosis requires a sharp intelligence of faith to discern what it is that all must hold for truth in unity, what each must preserve as part of legitimate diversity, and what can be left behind for the sake of harmony.

The way of learning and receiving has been proposed by the participants of an ecumenical meeting held in January 2006 at Durham University and Ushaw College in England, close to the hallowed resting place of St. Cuthbert. Cardinal Walter Kasper gave the keynote address and participated in the work.

It was a new initiative. Catholics were simply asking the representatives of their sister communities—Anglicans, Orthodox, Methodists, and others— what, in their view, Catholics could learn from them. The three days of conversations revolved around some principal issues of convergences and divergences: the role of the laity, the meaning of collegiality, the practice of primacy, and so forth.[1]

---

1. See Paul D. Murray, ed., *Receptive Ecumenism and the Call to Catholic Learning: Exploring a Way for Contemporary Ecumenism* (Oxford: Oxford University Press, 2008).

The inspiration came from Vatican Council II:

> Catholics must gladly acknowledge and esteem the truly Christian endowments from our common heritage which are to be found among those separated from us. . . .
>
> Nor should we forget that anything wrought by the grace of the Holy Spirit in the hearts of our separated brothers and sisters can contribute to our own edification. Whatever is truly Christian is never contrary to what genuinely belongs to the faith; indeed it can always bring a more perfect realization of the very mystery of Christ and the church. (UR 4)

Of course, any learning and reception should be done wisely, without endangering the substance of our faith or the specific diversity and beauty of our Roman communion. In truth, such enrichment on the Catholic side has already taken place; for example, we learned and received much in the field of biblical studies from the Protestant communities.

If we have become dejected by hearing the somber news about the ecumenical movement and if we were tempted to leave it as the two disciples left Jerusalem for Emmaus, the proposals coming from France and England show us new vistas. They may *open our eyes* to see new opportunities, *burn our hearts* with new hope (see Luke 24:31-32), and let us resume the work with a love that only the Spirit can grant.

CONCLUSION

The issue of Christian unity is mostly thought of—by believers and non-believers alike—as an internal matter for Christian communities. In truth, much more is at stake. Christ has come, has died, and has risen for the whole human family. In this immense work of redemption his church is called to play an indispensable role. It is the keeper of the good news. It is the eminent source of divine energy through the blessed play of sacred actions.

But the very sacrament of the Word, the community of Christians held together by the Spirit, is torn internally, and much of its energy is burned up by dissent. It is handicapped in announcing God's saving message. It is hampered in dispensing God's exhilarating graces.

In our days, the human family has an extreme need to hear the life-giving news and receive the infusion of fresh force—divine news and divine force. Never before has evil had so much power to put science and technology into its service. Violence is rampant in numerous places; it may even appear that God has abandoned creation and the Spirit is not moving over the face of the planet Earth—in contrast to what we read in the beginning of the Bible (see Gen 1:2).

The world needs a church that proclaims with one clear voice the message of peace—God's peace. But when Christians speak with discordant voices, how can anyone hear the one message of Christ? When Christians do not exchange a kiss of peace, how can they bring the peace of Christ to others?

There is no time to waste "for the creation waits with eager longing for the revealing of the sons of God" (Rom 8:19).

5

Reception of the Laws

An Exercise in *Communio*

Human laws are amphibious creatures: they live in two different worlds. They are conceived and created in the abstract world of the mind.[1] They are received and implemented in the concrete world of human history. Their passage from the first into the second means a radical change in their environment, a change that may alter their intended effectiveness. Thus, a norm conceived abstractly for the sake of justice may inflict injustice concretely;[2] unless, of course, equity (*epieikeia*, as Aristotle called it) comes to the rescue.

The two worlds, the abstract and the concrete, are organically linked: one could not be without the other. Yet each has its own nature and ways of operating.[3] In the first, perpetual essences are displayed in shining order; in the

---

1. See *Nicomachean Ethics* by Aristotle, Book 5.

2. Cf. the Roman adage *summum ius summa iniuria*, which could be, if not rendered, at least approximated in English as "consummate justice, consummate injustice." There is an irony in the play on the words *ius* and *in-iuria* that is easy to miss in translation: it is precisely the perfect application of the law ("right") that becomes an agent of injustice ("un-right"). Behind this adage there is the deep conviction that dominated Roman law in its formative period: laws are subject to a higher order of morality, the same conviction that helped to transform the rigid civil law into an equitable system. There was definitely a trend away from legal positivism in Republican Rome!

For some far-reaching references on this maxim (and others) see Detlef Liebs, ed., *Lateinische Rechtsregeln und Rechts-Sprichwörter* (Munich: Beck, 1982) 203. The book is a collection of more than 1,600 Latin maxims of jurisprudence, with their translations into German and notes on their origins, and also with references to articles, dissertations, and books written on them. This is a mine of information, besides being a "Book of Wisdom" in law.

3. There is a hint of the difference between theology and canon law: through theology the church seeks the understanding of the mysteries, all of course in the world of abstractions; through the service of the laws the church intends to shape its own life and the environment in which it exists, all in the world of concrete events. To acknowledge this difference is to give each of these disciplines its due, to purify them internally, and to liberate them externally from distorting interferences.

second, the existential energies of life are reigning. The overall priority, however, belongs to the world of existence because God is existence itself.[4]

The reception of laws takes place in the existential world, the place of concrete, particular, and personal events. There the people of God can turn an abstract, universal, and impersonal norm into a force of life that helps sustain and nourish the community.

For a helpful comparison, let us return to the example of the beautiful medieval cathedrals, first conceived in an abstract world. Initially they were no more than the dreams or the designs of the architects. They began to soar to the sky when the local people received the projects, that is, when the inhabitants of the cities and villages, the masons, the carpenters, the sculptors, the painters, the glaziers, and the thousands of load carriers started their work. They transformed the dreams into reality; they built the cathedrals. The process of building was the act of reception.

In the church, the lawgivers are like the architects. The law-abiding people are like the builders.[5]

The present reflections on the reception of the laws intend to unravel something of the ways by which the church is sustained through the service of the laws.

WHAT IS OUR QUESTION? WHY RAISE IT?

The question is then: How do laws move from the internal world of the mind into the external world of action, and how do they become a force of life therein? To find the answer should not be that difficult: after all, we are no strangers to the event. Whenever we obey the laws, we are receiving them. Rarely, however, do we pause and reflect on what is going on within us; still less do we attempt to give an account of the process. For this reason, let my discourse be not only a piece of exposition but an invitation as well, an invitation to look into ourselves and discover how we—we all as people—are mediators in turning abstract norms into forces of life.

---

4. This is a classical Thomistic position: the order of *esse* has priority over that of *essentia*. It is also the traditional Christian belief expressed in many ways in the Scriptures, one of them in Matthew's gospel: "Not everyone who says to me, 'Lord, Lord,' shall enter the kingdom of heaven, but he who does the will of my Father who is in heaven" (Matt 7:21). The divine judgment on a person's worth will be based on what happened in the concrete order; this is the primacy of the existential.

5. The point of this comparison is in stressing the primacy of existence: the cathedrals could never exist without the laborers, no matter how good the designs may have been. The living body of the church could never function without those who are putting into practice its norms, laws, and rules, no matter how well such directives are conceived.

Vatican Council II has certainly brought into the forefront the issue of reception, be it of doctrine, be it of norms of action. The Council stressed the role of God's people in the building of the church, and reception is very much part of that. Indeed, daily we are active players in the reception of the same council—with all the joy and pain that it entails. It is fitting that we should make an effort to articulate reflectively what we are doing instinctively.[6]

This articulation is warranted all the more as the conditions of our contemporary society are changing rapidly. The educational standards are moving upward in many nations; those in authority are less and less able to issue peremptory commands and obtain facile compliance. People, within and without the church, want to know the reason for a law; they want to understand the good that it intends to achieve; they want to implement it intelligently and freely. Such an attitude is no more than an assertion of human dignity, a stance that the church, no doubt, wishes to honor.[7]

For such reasons, the topic of reception is worthy of our attention.

WHAT DO WE INTEND TO ACHIEVE? WHAT SHOULD WE AVOID?

We wish to *discover* (not to invent) the normative pattern of the reception of laws in the church. Unless we are in possession of such an ideal, we have no measure by which we can judge the real.[8]

Because this normative image must be critically sound, right from the beginning a couple of unfounded theories and misconceived ideologies concerning the nature of canon law must be discarded.

There is the position of "canonical fundamentalism." It perceives the texts of canon law as carved into a stone, as the laws of some ancient nations are reported to have been: immutable, perpetual, and lifeless. For this theory, any suggestion that life may shape the law, or that intelligent and responsible interpretation can develop its meaning, is anathema. As ideologies do, this one too ignores history, history that shows how our canonical norms have evolved ever since the beginning of Christian ages.

---

6. In philosophical language we should say, let the focus be the subject, recognizing that in this case each one of us is the subject.

7. This is an interesting topic for a creative inquiry: How can the church (always a faithful trustee of divine revelation) best honor human dignity in its members? What kind of moral obligations exist, what sorts of legal norms could best serve this purpose? The underlying assumption of any such inquiry is that to honor the dignity of human persons is to honor God.

8. In other terms, we wish to understand what the correct pattern of reception ought to be, considering the specific nature of communication that takes place in the appropriation of the laws by the community. This is a theological and philosophical inquiry.

Canonical fundamentalism cannot explain the process of reception because it denies even the possibility of a process. It places the law outside human history, and makes it eminently inhuman for that.[9]

Another extreme position is "canonical relativism." For it, there is no such thing as the "truth of the law": a normative meaning implanted into the text by the legislator. The promulgated text is a mere point of departure that can be twisted and turned according to the wishes of the interpreter or the "operator." The theory opens a not-so-disguised door to anarchy.

Canonical relativism cannot give a sound explanation for the process of reception because in this theory there is nothing other than a process—with no permanent meaning holding its beginning and its end together. The law suffers from a lack of consistency and continuity throughout its life, from promulgation to implementation.[10]

In the Catholic canonical tradition there is not, there has not been, and there will be no room for either of these excesses. One could be just as destructive as the other. They need not detain us any further. A couple of cautionary remarks, however, are still necessary.

First, my inquiry is not intended to be exhaustive. There are many aspects of the reception of the laws that I shall not touch on, for instance, the past and present histories of receptions, the lurking danger of biased interpretations, the role of various sociological and cultural factors in the implementation of the laws, and so forth. These are important, but I wish to focus on the fundamental issue, namely: What should be the correct theological pattern of reception?[11]

Second, the fact that I focus on the process of reception should not be interpreted as a neglect of (or worse still, disregard for) the law-making process. Nor should my insistence on the power of God's people be taken as a denial

9. Today, after the Constitution on Divine Revelation (*Dei verbum*), when virtually the whole church peacefully accepts that there is a development in doctrine, not to accept that there can be a development in the interpretation and application of the laws is an indefensible position.

Helmuth Pree, in his well-documented monograph *Die evolutive Interpretation der Rechtsnorm im Kanonischen Recht* (Wien: Springer, 1980), has shown that from Gratian to Aquinas, from Aquinas to Suarez, and from Suarez to the present time (the three historical parts of his study), canon law kept evolving and interpretation has played a significant part in this process. It could not have happened in any other way since so much of canon law was customary law.

10. Such theory is vitiated by an underlying denial of authority that is not compatible with Catholic beliefs, besides being rooted in the Humpty Dumpty philosophy of "the words mean what I want them to mean."

11. This is, however, not a Platonic ideal. Plato's ideas were perfect and existed in a world that no human eyes could see. Here, our aim is to discover the most satisfactory (the best) pattern that is not only conceivable but achievable in our own existing universe. A great difference.

of the legislator's authority. My concentration is a methodological strategy, not a denial of the importance of other efforts and events. Besides, how could a cathedral ever be built without a designer? How could it be erected in an orderly way unless a clear vision guides the builders?

WHAT IS THE ENVIRONMENT OF THIS INQUIRY?[12]

The environment of this inquiry is the Roman Catholic Church.[13] Within this community of faith I wish to converse with those who belong to the same. In other words, I am not a detached observer reporting to neutral onlookers. My inquiry concerns business in the house of God: I wish my insights to be rooted in our Christian tradition and my affirmations transfused by faith.[14]

(For this reason, my explanations of the process of the reception of ecclesiastical laws will differ significantly from any account explaining the reception of the secular laws in a state. The ecclesial community is animated by the Spirit of God; the secular community is sustained by the prudence of the human spirit.[15])

In this living church, the reception of laws takes place in the *existential order* where the energies of life flow, where historical events succeed each other, and

12. Some background explanation to this question may prove useful. Theology can be done in two ways. In the first, the believer reflects (and reports) on the understanding of the mysteries of faith; in the other, a detached observer (unbeliever or believer abstracting from faith) reflects (and reports) on a religious phenomenon, on what others believe.

There is a radical difference between the two: in the believer the objective data of revelation blend with personal internal experience; in the observer the mind works with ascertainable external data only.

The merit of modern hermeneutical science is precisely that it has drawn the attention to the role of personal internal dispositions in reaching insights and formulating judgments. Classical theology has occupied itself a great deal with the so-called *loci theologici,* "places" where data for theological reflections can be found; they were all conceived as objective, independent of any "subjective" disposition. Hermeneutics has shown that accumulated experience in a person is "objective" (it exists) and inevitably plays its part in any intellectual discovery process.

By stating that my inquiry takes place in the "environment" of the church, I consciously distance myself from any approach that sees the world of religious (canon) law in the same way as it sees the word of secular law.

13. This in no way should be interpreted as some kind of ecclesiastical provincialism. It means simply that as far as my inquiry goes, in the immensely varied church of Christ, I am focusing on the Roman Catholic communion.

14. This is a hermeneutical stance for the composition of this inquiry and a clue for its interpretation. All that is going to be said should be ultimately rooted in an ambiance created by the Word of God.

15. This is the reason why I do not use "models" of reception. The reception of the ancient Roman law in the medieval Western Empire would not give much guidance for finding a normative pattern for the reception of ecclesiastical laws in our church of today.

where intelligent and free persons are called on to make responsible decisions. To use the image of building a cathedral: my observations do not concern the world of abstract designs, but the one where the stones are reached for, carved, and put together. I am interested in the practical art of building.[16]

At the same time I wish to keep in mind that the church is an *organic body* where we all are bound to each other in a variety of relationships. The lawgivers and the receivers are linked together: they are members and organs of the same body. Further, the givers are also receivers, and the receivers should cooperate in the process of giving.

This church, however, is *unfinished.* It is like a growing human being: to live, develop, and prosper, it needs to reach out for those things that can nourish its life—we call them values.[17] The purpose of laws is to prompt the community to appropriate those values; the reception of the laws is the process by which the community comes into the possession of the same values. (The laws speak of *intended* values; reception means the *acquisition* of values.)

The church is the beginning of the kingdom: it is *in via* toward its fullness. For this reason, it is a developing body, and everything in it, be it doctrine or discipline, participates in this expansive process.

WHO IS THE LAWGIVER?

In our modern church very little room is left for customary laws. For practical purposes,[18] the lawgiver for the universal church is the pope, and for the particular churches or communities it is the bishops and their synods at various levels.

To assess and correctly appreciate the lawgiver's role, we have to understand his position in the community, the task set before him, the divine assistance he can count on, and the scope of his activity.

His position in the community is that of God's steward (*epitropos* in the language of the New Testament: manager, governor) or that of God's "caretaker"

---

16. There is, though, a radical difference between building a cathedral and building the church. The former is made of stones and the product is an inanimate building; the latter consists of human persons and is growing into the kingdom of God.

17. The term "value" signifies throughout this study "a good thing in a positive relationship to a human person or to a human community." All created things are good in themselves, but not all of them are meant to contribute in the concrete order to the life and development of a given person, or of a given community. The concept of value includes relationship. A value could be internal to a person (such as skill, knowledge, virtue) or external (such as food, instruction, friendship). Canon law may impose an action in view of an internal or an external value.

18. One could say also "in ordinary circumstances." "Extraordinary circumstances" would be created by the convocation of an ecumenical council which, of course, would have legislative authority for the universal church.

(*oikonomos* in patristic language: entrusted with the household). He is inserted into the organism of the whole social body. As lawgiver he has no existence for himself. Whatever he has, including the special charism of his office, he has it for the sake of the whole. He operates from the resources of that body: the original divine revelation and the subsequent traditions are not exclusively his. The usual perception that sees the lawgiver as a solitary figure using his personal assets is doctrinally incorrect.

He belongs to the rest of the community as the head belongs to the body. Vatican Council I made this point forcefully when it stated that the infallibility of the pope (in defining a point of doctrine *ex cathedra*) is "the infallibility with which the divine Redeemer willed his church to be endowed" (see DS 3074). In other terms, the gift of infallibility is infused into, and rests in, the whole church, even when it is actuated (should it so happen) through the privileged ministry of the successor of Peter. Vatican Council II has confirmed this doctrine.

If that much is true of the supreme gift of infallibility, the "analogy of faith" postulates that "lesser gifts" as well, such as graces necessary for forming practical judgments and decisions for the welfare of the whole body, should also be present and diffused in the very same body. Saying all this does no more than stress the idea of *communio*, so much insisted on by Vatican Council II.

The task set before the legislator is to be of service to the people:

> For those ministers who are endowed with sacred power are servants of their brothers and sisters, so that all who are of the people of God, and therefore enjoy the true Christian dignity, can work toward a common goal freely and in an orderly way, and arrive at salvation. (LG 18)

This statement by the Council is not an idle phrase. It asserts that the needs of the community should command the operation of the legislator at every step he takes. He is in a paradoxical situation: because he is superior, he must obey. This obedience is the precondition of well-conceived commands. Gregory the Great understood this well when he assumed what has become the title of honor for the popes: *servus servorum Dei*, "the servant of the servants of God."[19]

---

19. Admittedly, we are still in need of construing a sound "theology of service"; it should bring a reevaluation of the relationship between superiors and subjects. A "superior" who accepts an office accepts to obey the needs of the "inferiors" who form the community. Hence the truth: good government is rooted in selfless obedience. Officeholders become corrupt when they begin to serve interests and values other than the ones for which the office was instituted.

An interesting question: Do office holders have a moral duty to give an account to the community about the use of the power? Since the community consists of intelligent and free persons, it seems fitting (it appears to be of good order) that the community should hear from the officeholders how *the common needs* are served; they are the community's needs, after all.

The divine assistance guaranteed to the successor of Peter and to the successors of the apostles is more discreet in practical matters—which include law making—than in doctrinal decisions. This is virtually a point of dogma that must not be lost from sight. An internal difference exists between an act of proclamation that tells the truth and an act of decision that imposes a course of action. In the first case, the guaranteed assistance of the Spirit goes as far as to prevent an official organ of the church from imposing a falsehood on the community; in the second case, *if doctrine is not involved,* there is no guarantee that an action lacking in prudence will be prevented.

God is protecting the purity of his own word. A false declaration could harm or destroy the revelation; a less than prudent action can indeed slow down the progress of the people toward the kingdom but cannot hurt or obliterate the truth.

The church, therefore, does not hold (and never did) that there is a divine guarantee that an ecclesiastical superior (including the pope and the bishops) will never fall short of the highest degree of prudence in practical matters. Historical facts prove abundantly the truth of this affirmation.[20]

There are consequences for the ecclesiastical lawgiver. First he must be careful not to ask for the same type of adhesion to practical decisions as to doctrinal declarations. Then he must constantly turn to the community in order to profit from all the practical knowledge and prudence found there. This "turning to the community" is not a legal obligation but of a higher order:[21] it is the duty imposed by faith to accept the organic nature of the church; it is an act of "obedience of faith" (Rom 1:5).

Limitation of divine assistance may postulate also that the community at large should play a greater role in the reception of the laws than in the acceptance of doctrinal instructions. This judgment is not about what is revealed truth but about what is good for the community here and now.

The scope of the activity of the legislator consists in issuing commands with authority in view of the acquisition of values by the community. This is the most that he can do. He has no capacity to create and give any of the values

---

Of course, I am not speaking of any legal accountability enforceable before a court: I am asking if there is a moral duty to honor the image of God in the subjects who are both intelligent and free.

20. Who would doubt today that in the fifteenth and sixteenth centuries, previous to the popular reformation movements in Europe, many "official" acts of the church fell short, and far short, of the ideal of Christian prudence?

21. The moral duty to consult can be made a legal obligation; see, e.g., the canons on the duty of the bishop to consult with his finance committee, with the council of priests, and the college of consultors (Canons 492–502).

the community needs; all he can do is prompt the people to reach out for them. He operates primarily in the abstract world of norms.

He hands over a design with the added strength of a command for the building of a cathedral.

WHO ARE THE RECEIVERS?

The receivers are the people of God: grace-filled, intelligent, and free persons. To know them better, however, we should inquire further: Who are they? What is their task? What divine assistance can they count on? And what is the scope of their duty?

The receivers are the community. Even the lawgiver is a receiver; he too must implement the law. This receiving community is already in "bondage"—by virtue of their baptismal covenant, they are bound to God and to the church into which they are incorporated.

Their task is usually described as that of accepting a new obligation imposed by a law. This way of speaking can obscure the substance of the truth. In the church (that is, the beginning of the kingdom) the source of all obligations is in a personal covenant with God. The people are bound to God. Consequently, they are committed to uphold the integrity of God's house.

The ecclesiastical legislator's power consists in imprinting a new specification on an existing obligation; in saying through his law what the particular object of a general duty ought to be.[22] The task of the people is to listen to the voice of the legislator with care, loyalty, and respect; they must keep in mind that they are members of a "hierarchical communion." Once the law is brought to their notice, they must enter into the process of reception.

The divine assistance granted to them is described in *Lumen gentium* 12:

> The universal body of the faithful who have received the anointing of the holy one (cf. Heb 13:15) cannot be mistaken in belief. It displays this particular quality through a supernatural sense of the faith present in the whole people when "from the bishops to the last of the faithful laity," it expresses the consent of all in matters of faith and *mores*. Through this sense of faith which is aroused and sustained by the Spirit of truth, the people of God, under the guidance of the sacred magisterium which it faithfully follows, receives no longer the words

22. A Christian is bound to God by a "from-person-to-person" obligation. All duties that emerge in his or her life are specifications of this unique overriding bond. (This is really the best key to understanding the nature of canon law: it specifies an already existing personal obligation in the faithful. For this reason, even if canon law looks like civil law and can be studied as civil law, it can never be received in the same fashion as civil law. A Christian subject always responds to his or her personal God.)

of human beings but truly the word of God (cf. 1 Jn 2:20 and 27); it adheres indefectibly to "the faith which was once for all delivered to the saints" (Ju 3); it penetrates more deeply into that same faith through right judgment and applies it more fully to life.[23]

Let us highlight a few points from this text, which contain important clues to assess and evaluate the role of the receivers:

- the people have a supernatural sense of faith and of *mores* (traditional practices);[24]

- this sense is given to them by the holy one of God (God's Spirit);

- this sense guides them to penetrate more deeply the doctrine of faith and helps them to form practical judgments as to how it should be applied to life.

The scope of their duty is to perform some action in the existential order: they are directed to reach out and effectively acquire the values necessary for the living community. They have to build the cathedral according to a pattern received. Their action, of course, will have to be in the existential order, an order that has an "ontological" priority.

WHAT IS RECEIVED? WHAT IS NOT RECEIVED?

Initially a piece of communication is received but not for the sake of mere information. It contains a law: a sentence in imperative mood, a command that points toward a specific action.

It cannot be stressed enough that there is a great difference between proclaiming doctrine and promulgating a command. When doctrine is handed over, the intent of the giver is an increase in knowledge; when a command is conveyed, his intent is the performance of an action.

It follows, therefore, that there must be a great difference between the reception of doctrine and that of law. In the former case reception consists in as-

---

23. Translation from *Decrees of the Ecumenical Councils*, Norman Tanner, ed., 2:858, with some changes that bring it closer to the original.

24. ". . . *consensum de rebus fidei et morum exhibet* . . ." says the original text. It echoes the definition of Vatican Council I on the infallible magisterium of the pope (DS 3074). *Mores* is often translated as signifying morality, as if the doctrine of Christian morality were not included in *fides!* The meaning of the two words so often joined together goes much further: it embraces Christian beliefs and practices; it signifies doctrine and customs. Thus, *mores* includes canon law, which it would not do if it referred to morality only. It follows that, by the doctrine of the Council, the faithful do have a supernatural instinct to understand, interpret, and implement legal norms.

similating the knowledge in an ever-expanding manner; in the latter case reception consists in narrowing the attention to one precise action and performing it.

Thus, the initial reception of the law triggers a process that ends when the community appropriates the value intended.

This value, however, was not contained in the law in any other way than intentionally. In other words, no real value is received when the community first accepts the law. The subjects will have to bring that value into existence by their action.

WHAT IS RECEPTION?

Above all, reception is a *dynamic process* brought forward by those immense energies that circulate in the community of the faithful. They are moved by a desire implanted by the Creator into the human heart to seek the good, and they are moved by the Spirit of God who has gathered them into one assembly, *ecclesia*, and is breathing life into their activities.

It is an *integrated process*. It consists of several stages that differ among themselves yet are organic parts of a whole. Each stage has its own function but they flow into each other and constitute an unbroken continuity. When I subject this "whole" to an analysis, I inevitably do some violence to a unity, but such a procedure is necessary for the sake of understanding it.

The first movement in receiving the law is to take cognizance of the norm that has been promulgated. There is a strong element of passivity in this (although no act of cognition can be merely passive), and it leads to the perception of the message, at least in its obvious grammatical sense.

The second movement is the quest for understanding: a search for the *why?* of the law. The object of this search is the value that has prompted the lawgiver to enact the norm—the value that the law intends to promote and support. To find it may require some detective work, but when it is found, the inner meaning of the law is revealed.

Not all the subjects are likely to engage in such an inquiry. Many prefer to trust the judgment of the legislator and feel no need to raise questions about the values behind the norms. This is a generally accepted attitude, even praised as virtuous. It is marked, however, by a built-in imperfection, a lack of understanding of the reason for law that can eventually lead to discontent and frustration.[25]

---

25. Cardinal Newman's remark concerning the consultation of the faithful in doctrinal matters is valid for canonical legislation as well. If the "teaching church," he says, follows a policy that neglects the consultation of the faithful in matters of doctrine and insists on the

The third movement in the process is its climax: the law meets the conscience of the receiver. It reaches that luminous part of the person where he or she is bound to God. There, a sovereign judgment will have to be made over the law, a judgment for which the person is responsible to his or her Maker and to no one else.[26]

This could be a routine event: as the law presents itself to the conscience, it is accepted in peace. Its harmony with the fundamental obligation to serve God is immediately detected.

In some cases, however, the conscience may sound an alarm: it finds a disharmony between the external rule and the internal drive to serve God. A conflict develops.

The source of the conflict need not be in the unsuitability of the law for the community; it could be in the individual circumstances of the person. (Remember: law is always an abstract, general, and impersonal norm; conscience always operates in the realm of the concrete, particular, and personal.) Be that as it may, before any action can be taken, the conflict must be resolved. There are ways and means to do that, either by invoking general principles higher than the law or by using correctives for individual circumstances, such as *epieikeia* (equity), *oikonomia* (economy), or dispensation.

In exceptional cases, there may not even be a doubt: the conscience responds to the law with a blunt *no*; then the process of reception stalls. This is not the right time to discuss and judge such occurrences. It is enough to state that they may occur. Each concrete case ought to be evaluated on its own merits.

The gist of this doctrine is the affirmation of the primacy of the conscience over the law: no Christian must hold otherwise. The Venerable John Henry Newman illustrated this dramatically in his famous remark: ". . . if I am obliged to bring religion into after-dinner toasts . . . I shall drink—to the Pope if you please—still, to Conscience first, and to the Pope afterwards" (*Letters and Diaries*,

---

duty of "implicit faith," *fides implicita* (his words) in the proclamations of the teaching church, then the process "in the educated classes will terminate in indifference, and in the poorer in superstition." *Mutatis mutandis*, a policy that neglects the consultation of the faithful in the law-making process, leaves them uninformed about the values the laws intend to promote and insists on obedience only, is likely to terminate in an alienation from canon law and in a disregard of the norms (cf. John Henry Newman, *On Consulting the Faithful in Matters of Doctrine* [Kansas City, MO: Sheed and Ward] 106). It follows that if at any time, as a matter of fact, there should be a widely spread hostility to canon law among persons who are otherwise dedicated to the church, it would be wise to ask if such a disposition has not been brought about by a lack of consultation.

26. This is the moment when the abstract, general, and impersonal norm encounters a judge (life, that is) who takes into account what is concrete, particular, and personal in the circumstances.

27:216). We can rephrase his sentence without altering its substance: "should the opportunity arise, we shall drink to conscience first, and to the law afterward." In stating this principle, the wise cardinal has really anticipated the doctrine of Vatican Council II (or, did he rather inspire it?): "It is through conscience that a human person sees and recognizes the demands of divine law" (*Dignitatis humanae* 3). If that much is true of divine law, how much more of human law![27]

The fourth movement follows after the conscience has accepted the law and has integrated its demands with the obligation that binds the person to God. The lawgiver's intention becomes the receiver's decision. He or she is willing to act, that is, to reach out for the value that the law wants. This is, before and above all, an *obsequium* to God, "honoring God," and only secondarily an act of obedience to the law.

The fifth movement on the part of the receiver is then the action itself, the implementation of the law in the world of concrete, particular, and personal events.

This passage of the laws through the conscience of the faithful is not the same as to subject the law to the ratification of the citizenry. A law promulgated by the ecclesiastical legislator is not subject to "ratification"; the movements described above belong to a deeper and personal level where the theological virtues reign supreme.

When implementation begins, a new period opens up in the life of the law.

27. This powerful doctrine could surprise the uninitiated. To grasp its portent, some further explanation is in order. There is autonomy in every human being: conscience presides over this autonomy. Even when God touches a person through grace, or when God conveys his Word, conscience must pass a judgment on what is happening. When conscience recognizes the source of the touch, or the truth of the Word, it directs the person to surrender and receive the transcendental gifts. Should the subject disobey, conscience will condemn him.

Whatever comes from the pope, be it a doctrinal declaration or a disciplinary imposition, it must knock at the door of the conscience: it cannot become part of the internal disposition of the spirit unless it is admitted. Of course, conscience may well tell a person to obey or else "lose integrity," which means to become a disoriented and internally divided human being.

We hold also that conscience must be well informed. This is not the place to prove that conscience must feed on knowledge; we all *know* that our own conscience often points toward a duty to gather information before a final decision. We know also that to evade this duty would be a way of resisting conscience and losing integrity!

Because of this priority of conscience, God will judge every single person not by any external rule (a law book) but by his or her fidelity to the dictates of conscience.

We see now why Newman gives such an absolute priority to conscience. Another way of grasping the meaning of his statement would be by reversing it and looking at the consequences. If we said "the pope first and the conscience second," the autonomy of the person, his or her intelligence and freedom, would be lost.

WHAT HAPPENS WHEN LAW AND LIFE MEET?

When the receivers begin to implement the law, they enter into a new venture: they are bent on changing and transforming this existing world. They may be doing so in a small scale; nonetheless, they are doing it.

They are far away from the world where the law was conceived, formulated, and promulgated. They are beyond the stage when the law was examined by their conscience. Their concern now is action in the existing world. Following the direction of the law (its original sense is not lost), they are intent on reaching out for values according to the initial design. The time for reflection is over; the time for "doing" is there.

This is a new moment in the life of the law. For the first time, the abstract norm meets the turmoil of concrete events. The law is tried in the crucible of life, as an old saying in jurisprudence goes.

The encounter may reveal a preexistent harmony between the demands of the law and the exigencies of life. When this happens, the two blend without a ripple and the community is enriched. It may well happen, however, that the norm does not fit well the conditions of life, and a conflict develops.

That such a conflict may occur should not be a surprise. After all, the legislator is human and fallible. He may not have foreseen all the consequences of his intended action. He could have even overrated the capacity of the community to appropriate an otherwise desirable value. (Wise legislation is always marked by good pedagogy.)

Our canonical tradition is aware that such an occurrence may happen and has a first remedy for it: let custom shape the law. The new Code echoes centuries of legal wisdom when it proclaims: "Custom is the best interpreter of laws" (Canon 27). It is equivalent to saying, "let life make its imprint on the law" because the forces of life generate customs; no custom was ever born from an abstract design.

At times, however, the conflict between the law and life may be so sharp that no custom can even out the differences. Thus, a law theoretically attractive may turn out to be concretely destructive of vital values.[28] There is no one

---

28. Even if the conflict of values may not be a frequent phenomenon, it should be adverted to in ecclesiastical jurisprudence so that when it occurs, we should be prepared to handle it. It arises when the law imposes an action for the acquisition of one value, but in the concrete order the same action is destructive of another value. A modern example in the United States would be the imposition of the requirement of a mandate on those who are teaching theological disciplines in a de facto Catholic university. In theory, there is a value in the institutional expression of *communio*. In practice, in several states such universities would become disqualified for public aid and the very existence of the institutions would be imperiled. (Then, of course, another question would arise: how to keep the *communio* intact and vital without the mandate.) Only a good perception of the hierarchy of values can help to resolve such conflict situations.

resolution of such a situation: the "implementers" and the legislator must work together to find the right course of action, which may vary from the prudent toleration of inaction to the revoking of the legislation.[29]

WHAT ARE THE SIGNS OF A WELL-ACCOMPLISHED RECEPTION?

This is a far-reaching question, but if we find the right answer, it should be a fitting way of rounding off our discussion. The issue could be put in this fashion too: are there signs by which we can recognize that the process of reception is going well and the law is on its way to becoming a vital force in the community? I am not looking for any theoretical evaluation of the content of a law or of its reception, but I wish to find *among the vital signs of the community* existential clues and hints that speak indeed of an "accomplished reception." I assume that the receiving community is well disposed toward the legislator and eager to preserve its own unity with him.

An easily recognizable sign that the reception is going well is peace in the community. The purpose of a law is always to bring order into the life and operations of a group. When the law does this, and does it in the right measure, the group responds with contentment. They have a sense of well-being: their vital energies flow unimpeded.

When the opposite happens—that is, the process of reception triggers restlessness, discontent, even resistance—in a well-informed, intelligent, and responsible community, it is time to examine anew the suitability of that piece of legislation.[30]

Christian people, however, do not live by social balances only. They live also by the Spirit who moves them in a mysterious way and gives assurance to them by the gifts of "love, joy, peace, patience, kindness, goodness, faithfulness, gentleness, self-control" (Gal 5:22-23)—all fruit of the Spirit. It should follow that such spiritual fruit could measure the success of reception. When, on the wake of the reception, joy and gladness abound, the concentration on faith, hope, and love increases, and the sense of unity is strengthened, then, the law is doing good service to the community. For good people to receive wise laws is a liberating experience.

---

29. See the thoughtful article by John M. Huels, "Nonreception of Canon Law by the Community," in *New Theology Review* 4 (1991) 47–61.

30. The remote source of inspiration for the practice of such discernment is in the "Rules for the Discernment of Spirits," in *The Spiritual Exercises of Saint Ignatius*, nos. 313–36.

Contrariwise, if a law brings sadness and sorrow, distraction from the exhilarating experience of God's presence, and undue preoccupation with temporal structures and institutions, it is time to question the law.[31]

For the sake of completeness, let me add that in a community ill disposed toward the legislator and torn apart by dissensions (that is, not living up to the Christian ideals), the impact of good laws is likely to be the opposite. Good laws will disturb the community since they interfere with the members' misguided intent; loose laws or the absence of needed laws will delight the subjects since they allow them to remain as they are—to their own destruction. The problems of such a community may be greater than what can be remedied by legislation.

Surely, such hints and clues are only signals that should be enough to initiate reflections but are not always enough to support firm conclusions. There could be other factors to be taken into account; in the existential order no two situations are identical.

These simple rules are really based on an ancient wisdom: those who walk in the light are friends of the light. In other terms, a community that needs peace in order to grow in faith, hope, and love is likely to be open to all laws that help it to fulfill their deepest aspirations.

IN THE LIGHT OF VATICAN COUNCIL II, IN WHAT WAY?

From the beginning, I intended to explore the process of reception in the light of Vatican Council II. This light played its part throughout my reflections, but it is fitting that as I come close to the conclusion of this topic, some insights of the Council should be more explicitly invoked and the validity of my conclusions tested by them.

The priority of the people of God. It is well known how the Council changed the proposed order of the chapters in the Dogmatic Constitution on the Church. Originally the hierarchy came first, the people afterward; in the final form of the document the people were given priority over the hierarchy. In retrospect it is easy to see the correctness of the Council's approach: the concept of "people" comprehends all, the hierarchy and the laity. Besides, a body is always prior to any of its members, even to the head.

The same spirit animates my discourse: the need to recognize the priority of the people of God in building the church. Yet the role of the hierarchy is in

31. There is a contemporary example: as the desire for the unity of Christians penetrated deeper and deeper into the consciousness of the Roman Catholic Church, many of the laws concerning "heretics" and "schismatics" began to cause distress among the faithful. When new laws were promulgated that took into account an existing partial communion, there was gladness among the people.

no way diminished. The pope and bishops are seen as the law makers in virtue of that "full, supreme, and universal" power that is described in chapter 3 of the same conciliar Constitution. They have the sacramental power (*dynamis, exousia*, in biblical terms; not just "jurisdiction" in the legal sense) to direct the activities of the household of God.

This power, however, is perceived by the Council as a duty to serve, exercised in obedience to the goals and needs of the community. This duty of obedience is of a higher order than any legal one; it is imposed by the sacramental consecration. My discourse intends to reflect this perception throughout.

The sensus fidei, *sense of faith of the people.* The Council describes how the people share in the prophetic office of Christ, how they have the capacity to penetrate their faith with correct judgment, and apply it more fully to daily life (see LG 12). If this ability has no role to play in the interpretation and implementation of the laws (which belong to the *mores*), then the Council made a futile statement with no bearing on the real world—which is absurd. We have a duty to uphold this particular teaching of the Council and to apply it to the reception of the laws.

By applying it, we also recognize and honor the sacraments of baptism and confirmation. Through them every Christian receives the seven gifts of the Holy Spirit; several of them, such as wisdom, understanding, knowledge, fortitude, and counsel, are certainly significant for the interpretation, reception, and implementation of the laws.

The historical character of the revelation. The Word of God, eternal and immutable, has entered into our universe, temporal and changeable. The Word has, therefore, a historical character; the Constitution on Divine Revelation (*Dei verbum*) leaves no doubt about that.

If that much is true of the Word itself, how much more it must be true of the human laws in the church! A law that is not historical would not be in harmony with the Word that became flesh: it would be a rigid shackle on God's people who should be alive and growing in grace and wisdom all the time.

The primacy of the conscience. The Council articulated clearly—with all due qualifications—the absolute primacy of the dictates of conscience. See the Declaration on Religious Freedom (*Dignitatis humanae*). Yet, the far-reaching implications of this doctrine concerning the obligations of the faithful within the church have received scant attention in theological writings. We can say with certainty that this teaching would be like "a noisy gong or a clanging cymbal" (1 Cor 13:1) if it did not apply to such a vital process in the church as is the reception of the laws.

The correct hierarchy of virtues. Innumerable texts could be quoted from the Council to show how it honors the supremacy of theological virtues: faith, hope, and charity. All other virtues are organically subordinated to these three.

Obedience to a human law (even if it is an ecclesiastical law) cannot be a supreme virtue: obedience can be authentic only when it functions in subordination to the theological virtues. To ask for blind obedience may even contradict the Scriptures: God's children are called to open their eyes, marvel at the mysteries, walk in the light, and flee all darkness.

CONCLUSION

In conclusion, first I wish to look back and recall the salient points of my discourse; then I want to reopen the issue of reception and suggest a topic for further study.

A brief summing-up. The crucial facts and events important to understand the process of reception of laws are the following:

* The church by its very nature is unfinished; to live and to prosper, it needs to acquire values.

* Laws are necessary to prompt people to reach out for values.

* Laws, however, being abstract norms, cannot give any value; people alone, in the existential order, can create or appropriate values.

* God's people are already in possession of the greatest value: they are committed to God. God alone must they serve.

* Every person, therefore, must insert the law's demand into the bond that he or she has with God. Conscience, with its supernatural sense, ought to be the judge.

* The positive judgment of the conscience should be followed in the concrete order by an appropriate action that implements the law.

* In the act of implementation, every law enters the crucible of life. If it passes that trial, the community will be enriched by the value that the law has intended in the first place.

The process of reception is completed.

Where do we go from here? What could be the next project? A suggestion: An ideal image of the process of the reception of laws is necessary, but it is not enough. What we need now is to find the concrete criteria to judge actual processes of reception as they take place in the existential order so that we can differentiate between authentic acts and aberrations. Inspiration for finding such criteria could be found in Congar's well-known work *True and False Reform in the Church*; the reception of a law, too, could be true or false. Relevant material could be gathered also from Newman's *Essay on the Development of Christian Doctrine*: more than half of the work is on the question of how genuine developments can be distinguished from corruptions. Throughout the history of the Christian community, laws were instrumental in bringing about reforms; developments in doctrine always had an impact on the legal life of the church. Hence the potential value of these two studies.

Now I return to the allegory of the ancient cathedrals, of their designers and builders. They had to work jointly; they could not do without each other. A designer alone could not lift a stone; masons and artists by themselves would have remained disoriented. The delicately balanced and breathtakingly beautiful buildings are the products of cooperation: designers and builders worked together.

Together the legislators and the people are called to build, and to take good care of, the house of God.

6

Law for Life
Canon Law after the Council

Let me sing for my beloved a love song concerning his vineyard:
My beloved had a vineyard on a very fertile hill.
He digged it and cleared it of stones,
and planted it with choice vines;
he built a watchtower in the midst of it,
and hewed out a wine vat in it;
and he looked for it to yield grapes . . .
What more was there to do for my vineyard . . . ? (Isa 5:1-2, 4)

To begin an exposition on the state of canon law with a poetic passage from the prophet Isaiah is unusual. But the allegory of the vineyard captures the inner core of my study. Yahweh built the vineyard, and he built a protective enclosure for it so that the life hidden in the vine may unfold and bring forth fruit. Isaiah sees a neat distinction between the external provisions (the clearing of the soil and the building of the watchtower) and the internal provisions (the wealth of the vines blessed with life) called to produce good wine.

The supporting structures of the vineyard—the walls, the beds, the paths, the watchtower—are meant to provide protection for the vines to grow and produce an abundant harvest of grapes. They are necessary but not life-giving. Life is in the plants and only there.

It is the same with the church. Structures, laws, and organizations are needed to provide an environment for life to unfold and expand. But life is in the people—only there and nowhere else.

Every allegory concerning the church, of course, only approximates a reality that is too mysterious to be expressed in our limited concepts and images. Nonetheless, the allegory of the vineyard, when judiciously applied, is a good way of representing the relationship between law and life in God's own domain that is the church.

THE THEME

The closer description of my discourse lies in the subtitle *Canon Law after the Council.* My inquiry asks: How far do our legal norms and practices measure up to the life-giving vision of the Council? How far does the Council and canon law form a unity in integrated harmony?[1]

In the search for the answers, I shall proceed in five steps:

The first part of my exposition could be called "due disclosure." In it, I wish to clarify some key concepts and expressions that will regularly occur throughout my exposition. My intention, however, is not to give standard definitions but to account for my insights concerning the understanding of certain theological realities and legal institutions. The second part will be a historical presentation of the state of the church and of canon law before the Council. The third part will focus on the event of the Council; it will be a provisional image since the significance of the Council is still unfolding. The fourth part will assess the state of the church and of canon law after the Council; it will be a report on a present reality in which we all are involved. The conclusion will be no more than an expression of hope: good ideas have a resilience that no human power can take away.

KEY CONCEPTS, CLUES TO UNDERSTANDING

The following concepts carry somewhat special (enriched) meanings in the context of this inquiry.

Church

What is the church? The church is all the people of God who are full with life-giving energy that wants to expand.[2] This energy leads them to fresh insights

---

1. For background, see *Sacrae disciplinae leges*, Apostolic Constitution by John Paul II, January 25, 1983, introducing the revised Code of Canon Law; AAS 75 (1983-II) VII–XIV.

2. Grace given by the sacraments, especially by the sacraments of initiation, should never be thought of as a static gift ("the person is sanctified") but as energy that presses and carries the person toward action—the speaking of the Good News and the building of God's kingdom.

about their faith and gives them strength for evangelical deeds. They are the recipients of God's gifts, distributed directly to the individual persons according to God's good pleasure. They all enjoy a fundamental equality flowing from the sacraments: baptism makes them God's children, confirmation makes them one in the Spirit, and Eucharist makes them one in the risen body of Christ. According to the testimony of Vatican Councils I and II, they are *collectively* the keepers of the sacred memory of the Christ event, and they *collectively* have the wisdom to build the church.[3]

At this point a couple of cautionary remarks are in order: First, no one can be fully integrated into the church unless he or she has living faith, firm hope, and active charity. To be a healthy organ in the body and to function well, a baptismal certificate or registration in a parish is not enough; sacramental life is essential. Second, we should be careful in using the term "laity," an expression that came into usage somewhere in the third or fourth century. There is no sacrament or sacramental in the church to confer on someone the "lay status." All are the people of God and remain so throughout their life. The clergy exist within the people and not as a separate class. An improper and uncritical use of the term "laity" has led to the less-than-sound theology that claims that the exclusive vocation of the laity is "to sanctify the world"—and then to leave the care of the church to the clergy. All who are people of God are called to build the church and sanctify the world. Not one of the letters from St. Paul (who was much concerned about "building the church") is addressed to the heads of the churches. Instead, they are addressed to the people. In his letters, we have an authentic source for the correct theology "of the people."

What are the "notes" (characteristics) of the church? We know that the church is one, holy, catholic, and apostolic; they are the notes we profess in the Creed.[4] The church has, however, other characteristics that are not in the Creed but are, nonetheless, true: it is *resilient* and it is *fragile*. The church is *resilient* due to divine assistance. The people of God, as long as they hold together in communion (and God will always preserve the unity of the "rest of Israel"), cannot lose the memory of God's saving deeds in Christ; nor can they lose the way to the kingdom. We believe in a resilient church. But the church is also *fragile*, because it is composed of human beings. Yes, the Spirit protects the assembly,

---

This is the kernel of the "theology of the people." We need parish councils not only for sound administration but also to channel the divine energy welling up in the parishioners.

3. For Vatican Council I see DS 3074, in particular the clause that states that the whole church is endowed with infallibility and indefectibility; for Vatican Council II see LG 12.

4. The notes point to the perfection of the eschatological church. We should add that the pilgrim church of Christ, while it is one, holy, catholic, and apostolic, is also divided, unholy, at times and in places too particular, and lacking of apostolic simplicity. The church is the assembly of sinners redeemed—on the way to being transformed to the image of Christ.

but the same Spirit does not take away the human frailty of its members. While, as a collectivity they cannot lose the apostolic message, no divine guarantee exists that in practical matters they will always observe the highest degree of prudence.[5] We believe in a fragile church.

Because ecclesiastical laws fall into the fragile dimension of the church, there are far-reaching consequences for the ecclesiastical legislator (who has his share in our common fragility): he needs help and advice here more so than in doctrinal matters. The same principle applies to the administrators who implement laws. Furthermore, scholarly interpreters and teachers of the laws have a special duty to examine the quality of the norms enacted and measure them by the theological values the norms are meant to serve. The position is sometimes put forward that the vocation of an academic lawyer is to exegete the law but not to evaluate. But this is a pernicious opinion because it deprives the legislator of needed help and support. It fosters irresponsibility and conformity when, for the welfare of the community, critical judgments are needed.

The assistance of the Spirit to the episcopate is different in matters that are doctrinal and practical. Ultimately the episcopate has the charism of infallibility, but it does not have the charism of supreme prudence.

Council

Below, I shall speak extensively of Vatican Council II. At this point, I wish only to draw attention to a distinction: every council in history brought forth "determinations" and was also an event. This distinction is particularly significant for Vatican Council II.[6] Determinations are objective propositions. We usually find them in collections titled "The Decrees of Ecumenical Councils." They may be doctrinal definitions or disciplinary regulations. But every ecumenical council was a historical event bringing a life cycle of the church to a closure and initiating a new one—an end and a beginning. Beyond their teaching function, the intellectual enlightenment of the church, councils always (or mostly) left an existential impact on the church that sometimes reverberated for decades or centuries.

---

5. It should not be assumed that the mark of the Spirit is absent in the legal system, or that some laws do not reach a high degree of prudence. Such an assumption would be incorrect—or downright silly.

6. There is nothing unusual in distinguishing between "doctrine" and "event." We keep interpreting the teaching of Jesus (doctrine) in function of his resurrection (event); the two mutually support and enlighten each other. We have a vast literature over the doctrine of the Council; far less has been said about the nature of the event. The texts alone cannot give us a full comprehension of the significance of the Council.

The proclamations of Vatican Council II have been, and will be, debated for a long time to come. Less attention is being paid to the Council as an event.

Theology

In this exposition the term "theology" means more than the art and craft of expounding the doctrine of faith into well-chiseled concepts and precise propositions. While such mental skill and agility is certainly needed in the church, the true foundation of any theological enterprise is in wisdom that speaks of ineffable mysteries apprehended by faith. Such wisdom should play a principal role in discovering Christian values that the community should appropriate. This is to say that an intuitive *sensus fidei*, or a "supernatural instinct," should be numbered among the sources of canon law.[7]

Canon Law

In colloquial conversations the term "canon law" is used—and abused—in several senses. At one end of the gamut, the speaker may be referring to petty regulations for the vexation of the faithful; at the other end, he may have in mind the God-given structures of the church. Authentic canon law, the compound of ecclesiastical laws, is between these extremes: it is not petty nuisance and it is not divine ordinance. It is a necessary human instrument, in a divinely founded community, to bring good balances into the operations of the group. It is also known as "ecclesiastical law."

Such an instrument is indispensable. No community, not even a community of God's children, can function without good order.[8] Further, no spiritual charism given to an assembly can survive in the vicissitudes of history unless it is supported and protected by legal structures and norms.[9]

The best definition of canon law (ecclesiastical law) is given by its purpose. It is a system of structures and norms to secure freedom for the people so that

7. Cf. LG 12: "The people unfailingly adheres to this faith, penetrates it more deeply through right judgment, and applies it more fully in daily life." This is briefly the reason why there should be room in the church for customary law.

8. There is order even in the holy Trinity: the Son proceeds from the Father, and the Spirit from the Father and the Son.

9. To accept the church spiritual but to reject the church institutional does not make sense within the Christian dispensation: it runs counter to the dynamics of the divine initiative in the incarnation. If a spiritual movement does not become "earthly" in visible structures, it is bound to pass away; history proves this abundantly. As we humans cannot be pure spirits, a human community cannot be purely spiritual.

they can receive, without impediment, the gifts of the Spirit. *And* it is a system of structures and norms to secure freedom for the Spirit to dispense, without impediment, God's gifts. The dignity of the ecclesiastical legislators exists in that they are called to create freedom for the citizens of God's kingdom *and* for God's Spirit. An awesome task.

Once freedom is created, life can sprout and unfold.

The Relationship between Theology and Canon Law

A question often raised is: How do theology and canon law relate to each other—which one has priority? The answer is that the question is somewhat ill conceived. Each has its own priority, but they must operate in organic unity—each retaining its own characteristics.

Theology operates on the abstract level. It has priority at the planning stage; it determines a value to be appropriated; it gives meaning to the law. Canon law operates on the concrete level. It provides norms of action in the existential order; it contributes directly to the building and well-being of the kingdom. While a vision must precede every reasonable action, a vision remains within the realm of theory. When a command for an action is issued, it intends to shape reality. And reality has its own God-given priority.

For this reason structures and norms cannot be handled lightly. They have an excellence that no theory can possess: they deal with existence. The actual building of a house has its own priority over the blueprint of the same house. In the church, canon law has an importance that no theory can match. It deals with the real existing social body. But a law not grounded in a value is like a house built on sand; it is bound to collapse.

The very question of priority is a misconceived query: there is one single process from vision to action, the parts build the whole. The meanings of theology and canon law are well understood when their relationship to each other is correctly understood.

Conversion

The concept of conversion will repeatedly return and may cause confusion. For this reason I wish to stress that, as a rule, I use the term not in the sense of abandoning the old faith and turning to some new fantasies, but in the sense of a "turning around" *within the framework of our Tradition* and reaching a deeper intelligence of faith and a wiser path in the obedience of faith.

My conceptual clarifications—a sort of *apologia* for giving a special sense to common terms and expressions—are now concluded.

Before entering into the historical part, however, a disclaimer is useful to dispel any misgivings should they exist. Nowhere in this exposition do I intend to be either conservative or progressive; my aim is to draw conclusions from verifiable evidence, or, to tell a story to the best of my capacity subject to completion or correction as new evidence arises or as we reach better insights into the available data. To be, as a matter of principle, either conservative or progressive is to confess an ideological prejudice that neither faith nor reason should tolerate.

BEFORE VATICAN COUNCIL II

The State of the Church before the Council

On the eve of the Council the church was bursting with divine energy, but lacking balance in its human operations. Virtually all the local churches and the people of God at large were reduced to varying degrees of passivity.[10]

Individual dioceses were allowed little initiative; the non-ordained faithful (I prefer that term to "laity") were not entitled to proclaim the Good News without a mandate from the hierarchy. The commonly held "official" doctrine was that the priests received their power "to feed the flock" from the bishop. And the bishops received their power to govern from the pope.

An understanding of the church's constitution—never defined as a matter of faith, yet operative in conceiving laws, issuing administrative orders, and setting policies—reigned: God designed the church in such a way that all good things, especially intelligence of faith and prudent decisions, should descend from above, from the person of the pope, the Vicar of Christ.

Within this understanding there was little space for creativity at any lower level, the level of the non-ordained, of the priests, and of the bishops. While the church may have been rich in energies, the restrictive structures and norms left little room for their activation.

The State of Canon Law before the Council

Please recall the principle that canon law (ecclesiastical law) is within the fragile structure of the church and that the legislator is not indefectible in prudential matters.

---

10. Ever since 1870 when the pope became the "prisoner of the Vatican," a new cult of the person of the pope began to emerge. In earlier times when Catholic people made the pilgrimage to Rome, they went there "to visit Peter and Paul," to do homage to the apostles. Modern pilgrims go to Rome "to see the pope." The visit of diocesan bishops *ad limina apostolorum* is widely perceived by all concerned as a visit *ad limina Pontificis*. Of course, it is right and just that believing people should show due respect for Peter's successor, but no "cult of personality" in a secular sense is becoming for God's people—it is not the style of God's court.

This is not to demean canon law. It has been doing and is doing an immense service to the church. The Code of 1917 established a concordance among discordant canons. It brought order, clarity, and legal security to the life of the community. So did and does the Code of 1983. Such praise has been voiced many times by prelates and scholars. I concur wholeheartedly. The system, however, was not and is not without problems.

Canonical jurisprudence has lost its vital link with theology; it became victim of "canonical nominalism."

The late Gérard Fransen, a much-respected professor of history of canon law at the University of Louvain-la-Neuve, was the first to recognize and explain how the disease of positivism came to affect canon law. In 1564, after the Council of Trent, to safeguard the integrity of the Council's decisions, Pope Pius IV forbade the publication of any "commentaries, glossaries, annotations, scholia, or interpretations of any kind concerning the Council's decrees."[11]

This was the beginning of "canonical nominalism," to use Fransen's expression. Canon lawyers had to content themselves with the task of paraphrasing the official documents without bringing any inquiring spirit into their work. With one stroke, that is, with one Pontifical Bull, the great tradition of "raising questions" that animated research in the Middle Ages was terminated. The method of Magister Gratianus who sought justification for every canon, the playfully serious method of *sic et non* invented, practiced, and taught by Abelard, and the incisive inquiries through alternating denials and affirmations by Aquinas were declared out of bounds. It was not the business of canon lawyers to search for values behind the canons. Unity, a value, had its own exorbitant price.[12]

As a result, for some four hundred years canon lawyers, without realizing what they were doing, operated within the narrow boundaries of a kind of legal positivism—well before the secular philosophers invented and professed it. First, they did it by imposition; then they continued by sheer force of habit and tradition. For proof, please consult the standard manuals from before Vatican Council II with the following question in mind: Just how many times do the authors critically examine the laws or the laws' connection with the

11. See Gérard Fransen, "L'application des décrets du Concile de Trente. Les débuts d'un nominalisme canonique," in *L'Année canonique*, vol. 27 (1983) 5–16; also DS 1849.

12. A reasonable and legitimate question: Why is there throughout the Catholic Church so much aversion to canon law? A tentative answer: because our people, blessed with a sense of faith, instinctively sense that some (many?) of our laws are not in the service of values of higher order.

foundational values of our Christian tradition?—as such values are evinced in the Scriptures, patristic literature, pronouncements of the great councils, and so forth. The manuals will speak for themselves.[13]

Canon law has become static, ahistorical, and near inimical to development.

Every legal system needs stability; without it the community suffers from uncertainty. But every legal system must be aware of the flow of history around it and have ways and means of introducing changes. If not, the system becomes a rigid monument, not a life-supporting instrument. We all know the principle "change in the law is odious," *mutatio legis odiosa*. We know equally well that if a law is not in step with history, it becomes irrelevant—or odious. Thus, laws need stability but also flexibility. Virtue is in the right balance, and the balance may need to change with changing times.

The two great legal systems of the West, classical Roman law and English common law, were born in and shaped by historical communities. The developing structures and norms responded to the emerging needs of the society. Laws are an integral part of our continually developing humanity.

The quest for order in the Christian church was also a response to the dynamics of history, to events within and outside the community. Canon law cannot be otherwise. It cannot be a set of rules carved on an immutable monument that successive generations may read but never regard as an organic part of their life. Every legal system must include provisions for the ongoing renewal of the law.

Civic communities avoid this problem. They have ongoing legislatures sensitive to the needs of the community. In the church we have the Code, but, in practice, no organism endowed with the specific task of detecting emerging needs and proposing changes. Serious problems remain unresolved, tensions develop; these tensions lead to crises, and finally the situation explodes.[14]

13. I recall vividly the first lecture given to the entering students (virtually all graduates in theology) in 1954 by the Dean of the Faculty of Canon Law at the Pontifical Gregorian University. He warned them: "You have learned in theology that the 'authorities' are the Scriptures, the Fathers of the church, the Doctors of the church, and so forth. You must forget all that. In canon law they are not authorities." The Dean merely voiced a common conviction then current among canonists.

14. This is exactly what happened when the crisis of sexual abuse descended on the church. It was coming for some time, and there was no adequate preventive legislation. A sensible system of the "visitation of the dioceses" by outside observers able to interview the people, the clergy, and the bishop separately could have discovered the problems much earlier. After their report to a higher authority, necessary preventive or remedial measures could have been taken.

Canon law has cut itself off from secular (human) wisdom.

Philosophy of law and jurisprudence are human sciences. Canon lawyers, just like secular lawyers, ought to cultivate them.

Ever since the Renaissance, humanistic secular jurisprudence has made immense strides in such matters as freedom of conscience, respect for human rights, impartial courts, speedy administration of justice, responsibility for the common welfare, and so on. Canon law remained mostly untouched by such developments; it remained attached to late scholasticism. Again, please consult the manuals on "Philosophy of Law" used before the Council: they are innocent of modernity. On the basis of knowledge gained from them, no one could carry on an intelligent conversation about the law with a well-intentioned contemporary secular thinker.

VATICAN COUNCIL II

Every council is an end and a beginning: it concludes an era and opens another. Vatican Council II was no exception. It was a turning point in the church's history. Yet, it had a particular character. It was more oriented toward the future than any other council before.

The Council as an Event

The Council was an event of conversion. To identify the extent of this conversion is not difficult. The point of departure of its work, *terminus a quo*, can be found in the textbook-type preparatory schemata and in the unimaginative proposals submitted by bishops and others before the Council. The point of arrival, *terminus ad quem*, is found in the final documents of the Council. Such documents, however, are merely witnesses of a deeper "turning around" that happened in the minds and hearts of the participants.

Let me add immediately and forcefully that *no one can appropriate the meaning of the Council unless he goes through the same process of conversion.* It is not enough to achieve an intellectual understanding of the texts. It is not enough to implement an intellectual position through new policies and ordinances. To appropriate the Council means to enter with mind and heart into a new horizon; it is to move out of the Tridentine environment and start living in an, until now, unknown environment. There are many who interpret the conciliar texts. There are also many who miss the living event.

To recall the allegory of Plato's cave can be helpful here. There are interpreters who received the documents in the cave and continued to interpret them in the cave. However, the documents were written outside the cave, in plain sunshine,[15] and they can be properly explained only in that blessed world illuminated by the sun. To quote Plato is not inappropriate: he is describing the behavior of human persons in various environments and the church is composed of human persons! He was one of the first to discover and exploit the sophisticated science of hermeneutics.

Once we realize that the Council was an event of conversion, we can understand the struggles during the Council. It was not just an academic debate. Further, we have the key to understanding the church's history after the Council. In these decades the whole Roman Catholic communion has been in the throes of a conversion process.

The Council Fathers were called to move into a new field of vision where they had to think and act in a different manner. So are we. Such transition or transformation is always painful; it means to leave behind the security of the known and enter into the insecurity of the unknown. The move is not purely external, like settling down under a new roof, but involves an internal change in our personality. We must cease clinging to our familiar habits of thoughts and operations and make room for new thinking. In the case of the church, we must make room for a newly fashioned community.

Behind the ideological battles witnessed by the speeches at the Council, visceral fears also played a role. To say so is not to reduce the conciliar debates to some silly psychology. It is simply to state that the participants were not only believers, but human beings.

Let us not hide an additional problem. The insights of the Council are so penetrating and far reaching that they can be grasped only slowly—even for those who took part in it. The meaning of the Council continues to unfold in our minds and hearts—travelers tend to understand their experiences only after they have completed their journey. To work on the unfolding of the mystery remains the task of the coming generations.

The Council as an event of conversion took place in the minds and hearts of the participants slowly and painfully, over the seasons of four years. The principal protagonist of this event was the gigantic figure of Pope John XXIII—*il papa buono,* "the good pope," as he became known worldwide. And I believe his stature will again increase.

When John XXIII convoked Vatican Council II, he reversed a trend of nine hundred years of centralization.[16] He confessed he was "inspired" to do so. He

---

15. It took some time, and some pain, for the majority of the Council Fathers to get there, but they made it.

16. One is reminded of the exultant cry of the Psalmist: "The sea looked and fled, Jordan turned back" (Ps 114:3). Pope John XXIII was certainly exultant in his speech from the

did it single-handedly, notwithstanding "prudent advice" to the contrary.[17] He knew there were problems with the church. He could have decided on a series of encyclicals instructing the people what to do. After all, he was the supreme teacher.

He did the opposite. He wanted to be a learner. He called on the universal episcopate for help, and the bishops came from every corner of the world. First, they were bewildered, and then they understood the pope's intent. Finally, they lived up to the call and created a new type of Council never seen before.[18] They, *as a college* that was aware of its supreme, full, and universal power, reversed a current coming from the depth of past centuries. They opened the gate for a new tide of energies.

It is no wonder that Vatican Council II does not fit easily into any category of councils. It was convoked in relatively serene times to bring about an *aggiornamento*, an "update" to the church. It was called not to destroy but to build and refresh the permanent core of our tradition with new insights.

Because Vatican Council II was so unusual in its convocation, operation, and achievement, its reception by the universal church cannot be but slow. It calls for the conversion of the entire Roman Catholic communion.[19]

Canon Law at the Council

On January 25, 1959, at St. Paul's basilica, John XXIII named three projects that he intended to initiate and promote as organic parts of his *aggiornamento*: a diocesan synod for Rome, an ecumenical council, and the revision of canon law. Events progressed in that order. The diocesan synod for Rome was held and concluded in January 1960. The Council was convoked and opened October 11, 1962. The work for the revision of canon law was initiated on March 29, 1963, when the pope appointed a commission of thirty cardinals, twenty-one of them from the Roman Curia.

---

window of his study on the evening of the opening day; in his joy he asked the mothers to bring his caresses to their children. He foresaw a far-reaching impact of the Council.

17. This trend of centralization led the Western branch of Christianity further and further away from the Eastern one; the Eastern churches continued to operate collegially on the basis of the ancient doctrine of synodality.

18. The bishops began to grasp the pope's deepest intent when, a few weeks into the Council, they started to vindicate their own right to compose the documents. The voice of the universal episcopate—muted for so long—was heard again in the church. The Council was coming to life; or life was (exuberantly) welling up in the episcopal college.

19. The receptions of the great councils were never instantaneous; those of the councils of Nicea, Chalcedon, and Trent were particularly slow.

As far as I know, the theme of "canon law at the council" has not attracted the attention of any researcher. Yet, such a history holds an important clue to the understanding of the postconciliar development of legislation.[20] A detached and detailed study of canon law after the Council is certainly due.[21]

AFTER THE COUNCIL

The State of the Church after the Council

In trying to sum up the history of the postconciliar era, an image comes to mind: the image of two mighty rivers—surging from distant sources, each full of energy—flowing toward the ocean and at some point colliding. There is turbulence, on a mighty scale.

In the church there was a current that originated some nine hundred years ago and was nourished and reinforced over the centuries to the very eve of the Council. It created its own ethos. The center was active, and the people at large led an existence of quiet passivity. People were given little responsibility and they were directed toward seeking their salvation through blind obedience.

Then Vatican Council II generated another current. Without destroying or harming the papacy as "the center of unity," it shifted the balance. It recognized

---

20. Anecdotal history is just that: anecdotal. Its value is limited. With this proviso, I wish to recall a conversation during the Council that I had with Msgr. Alexandre Renard, then bishop of Versailles, later Cardinal Archbishop of Lyon. I mentioned that the reception of the Council would depend largely on the new canon law. "Will the Council do anything about it?" I asked. His response was swift and to the point: "I do not care about canon law"; it is even more to the point in the original French "*Je m'en fiche de droit canonique.*" Question: Have some bishops (the Council?) failed to realize the existential role of law to create the freedom necessary for the reception of the Council?

21. In this context, however, for the sake of historical accuracy and completeness, it must be recorded that one group displayed an unusual perspicacity. Immediately after the Council, Opus Dei would participate very little in the new organisms created in the Vatican as an outcome of the reformist aspects of the Council (Secretariats for unity, for non-Christians, for nonbelievers, council of laypersons, etc.), which were primarily occupied by the representatives of the most "open" or "advanced" currents, who were enjoying a wave of euphoria at that moment. These same "progressive" sectors, however, undervalued the importance of another area, which they found unattractive and did not want to devote any time to: canon law. Opus Dei, on the other hand, fostered the cultivation of this discipline; the University of Navarre became the seedbed for a school of canonists, and from the very moment of the creation of the Committee on the Revision of Canon Law, Opus Dei took an active role in it. For a detailed report see Joan Estruch, *Saints and Schemers: Opus Dei and Its Paradoxes*, trans. from the Catalan (Oxford: Oxford University Press, 1995) 206. Today Opus Dei has a flourishing faculty of canon law in Rome as part of their Pontificia Università Santa Croce.

God's gifts dispersed in the community and asked each person to accept shared responsibility and exercise creativity for the benefit of the whole.[22]

After the Council the two currents met and clashed. The result was, and still is, turbulence among God's people.

The State of Canon Law after the Council

For canonists the greatest event after the Council was the publication of the revised Code of Canon Law in 1983 with the Apostolic Constitution *Sacrae disciplinae leges*. Ever since, the norms contained in the Code (and the subsequent enactments complementing them) have been shaping the church and directing its operations. The new Code is a significant improvement over the old one. But has it brought us a substantial *aggiornamento*?

To come to a fair judgment, let us return to the shortcomings that existed before the Council and see how far they have been remedied.

Centralization

If Pius XI *redivivus* visited the church today, he would find little new evidence for changing his judgment that "the head is very large, but the body is shrunken."[23] The "episcopal synod" that Paul VI initiated to identify critical issues in the life of the church and provide some episcopal leadership has become a mere consultative body to the pope (and the Roman Curia) within well-defined and rather narrow limits.[24]

22. We hear much about the imaginary case of Conservatives v. Liberals in the church; cf. above. The labels are misconceived, misplaced, and misleading. Today's "conservatives" are mostly clinging to convictions and habits developed mainly after the Council of Trent; rare among them are those familiar with the church of the first millennium, and even rarer those who wish to return to its practices. They who in common parlance are called "liberals" hardly form a cohesive group. Many of them are simply searching honestly for the correct practical implementation of the conciliar vision. Others are "free thinkers" of sorts; they want to propagate the Council's vision but do not have enough knowledge to do so within the balancing parameters of the Tradition; they easily fall into unacceptable excesses. With some simplification it is fair to say, though, that the contemporary fight between the conservatives and the (faithful) liberals is between the "Tridentines" and the followers of Vatican II.

23. See chap. 3, pp. 36–37.

24. In connection with the papacy there is a thorny issue, rarely pondered by theologians. We hold as dogma that the pope is the bishop of a diocese (Rome) with the rights and duties that such an office involves; he is a diocesan bishop, but because he succeeds Peter, he has also the office of primacy. In other terms, according to Catholic belief, there is not a "super-bishop" in the church. The pope has the primacy because he is a local bishop, of a privileged place, of course. What is the full meaning of such an arrangement? What does it mean in the practical

The episcopal conferences exist and operate in the shadow of the Roman Curia; they have little room for any creativity. Even the limited freedom granted to them by the Code of Canon Law has been reduced by the Apostolic Constitution *Ad apostolos suos* to the point where the exercise of their mandate to teach is virtually impossible and where every decision needs Roman consent— disguised under the name of "review."[25]

Admittedly, since the Council, the role of the non-ordained persons ("laity") in the internal life of the church has visibly increased. They work in chanceries, ecclesiastical courts, parish councils, and other ministries. For this we should rejoice. Yet, paradoxically, the new Code drew a sharper line between the ordained and the non-ordained than any law or custom did before. The non-ordained cannot share the power to govern, *munus gubernandi*, not even by delegation. This excludes them from significant decision-making processes that affect the life of the church: a restrictive innovation that ignores a contrary tradition.

Legal positivism, canonical nominalism

In the years after the Council and before the promulgation of the new Code, there was voluminous "wisdom literature" about the role of law in the church. Presently, an increasing number of textbooks are slipping back to the comfortable position of never asking about a law's link to theological values. Canonical science is drifting toward an exegesis of the texts that would satisfy the Tridentine censors. No wonder the respect for law in the community is not increasing.

The acceptance of a historical existence

We have stability in canon law for the Code provides well for it. But unlike civil communities, we have no means built into the system for the renewal of our laws. We do not have an organ specifically entrusted with the particular task of watching great cultural movements, assessing the emerging needs, and

---

order? Why did the early church decide not to follow the usual secular pattern of having one "general supervisor," with no other burden attached? A topic worthy of further exploration, it has its importance not only for the internal government of the church but also for the progress of the ecumenical movement.

25. It is interesting to note that the doctrine of episcopal collegiality underlying and defining the present status of episcopal conferences is virtually identical with the position of a minority at the Council that claimed that *effective* collegiality exists only when an ecumenical council is in session or in analogous circumstances when the bishops, although dispersed physically, are called by the pope to act in a collegial manner. The majority that voted for collegiality had a much richer understanding of it based on the traditional doctrine of synodality that was operational even in the Western church throughout the first millennium.

proposing changes in the law accordingly. We let tensions develop, allow one crisis to follow another, and tolerate breakdowns before we reach for the remedy of prudent legislation. Since the church is embedded in an evolving universe and is an integral part of human history, it must be equipped to handle changes.

For example, the inability of our legal system to respond to the sex abuse crisis in a prompt, fair, and efficient way is an illustration of its rigidity. Super diocesan institutions, such as episcopal conferences, regional synods, or a "universal synod" would be eminently suitable for identifying problems and proposing new legislation.

Learning from secular sages

In the Middle Ages, the study of canon law went hand in hand with the cult of civil law: they shared whatever wisdom they could find. The Reformation and Enlightenment put an end to this partnership, and canon law remained alone and did not benefit from the significant progress in legal wisdom achieved in civic communities. To a large extent, this continues to be the case today.

A comprehensive critical study of the relationship between the values asserted by the Council and the postconciliar legislation remains to be done. We are far from having accomplished an authentic *aggiornamento* of our canon law. Nevertheless, I can think of two significant initiatives toward progress that are immediately feasible. One is in the realm of theory and the other in the field of practice.

1. In preparation for a future revision of the Code of Canon Law, we should have a group of competent and dedicated theologians and canon lawyers that work closely together to identify afresh the theological values that need legal support. The result of their study could be submitted to the (future) pontifical commission charged with reviewing the whole system. If such a preparatory work is well done, and if it is made public, it would be difficult to ignore it. Its content would give it authority. That is a worthy challenge for a professional Canon Law Society.[26]

2. In the field of practice, the reform should start with the administration of justice. We should make our courts autonomous (as much as possible

---

26. The work would have to be very focused and disciplined, but it could be done in a relatively short time. It would be an immense service to the church, in this clear and simple form never done before.

without hurting any dogma) and start dispensing fair and speedy justice. The doctrine of sacramentally conferred episcopal power need not exclude operational independence. What an asset it would be for a new evangelization if the Catholic Church had the reputation of being exemplary to the nations in the administration of justice!

CONCLUSION

The Council ended in 1965. However, the internal struggles that over four years animated the meetings and the intermissions have not ended. They continue in the Roman Catholic communion at large. The Council Fathers grappled with the process of conversion as the church does today. It is more than a human event: the forces of the Spirit that once moved the Council are "disturbing" the entire church today. They are disrupting earlier attitudes and habits, and, yes, causing turmoil. We should have been able to foresee this, but we did not.

To live in our contemporary church is like being called to be an actor in a drama of immense proportions. The scene extends as far as the community has spread. The main theme of the play, designated by the Council, is to liberate insights and energies in every part of the church for the benefit of all. The gifts of God should be manifest and put to good use so that all may rejoice in a divine abundance. We are not spectators of this drama, comfortably watching the play. We are called to be participants. We are exposed to the experience of conversion, to the agonies and ecstasies of a passage from the familiar into the unfamiliar.

This drama is not likely to end anytime soon, but the outcome can hardly be in doubt. If the Spirit initiated the Council, the same Spirit will accomplish the work in ways that we cannot anticipate.

For the time being, the wise Rabbi Gamaliel is of good counsel:

> If this plan or this undertaking is of men, it will fail; but if it is of God, you will not be able to overthrow them. You might even be found opposing God. (Acts 5:38-39)[27]

27. This chapter ends on a note of hope and on hope well grounded: we have seen the beginning of a process initiated at the Council by the Spirit. It was right and just to expect that the initial divine gifts will unfold. Yet, a question may linger in the mind of the reader: What if the fulfillment of the promise is delayed and continues to be so? What should we do? The response is that the promise of the Spirit is alive and strong but the time of its fulfillment has not been revealed to us. *We must not depart from Jerusalem* [that is from the church] *but must await the promise of the Father* (cf. Acts 1:4). God will speak and act in his own good time.

7

Justice in the Church
The Legal Wisdom of Our Age

Today, all over the face of the earth, there is a deeply felt hunger for justice and a persistent cry demanding respect for human persons and their rights. The church sensed this hunger and heard this cry; it responded with solemn pronouncements and became a forceful advocate of human dignity.[1] Nations are attentive and listening, but they are also watching to see if the deeds of the church follow its words.

It is fair, therefore, that we should examine our ways of dispensing justice so that in such matters the church shall be light to the nations, *lumen gentium*, as it is called to be. In this spirit, I offer the following reflections. These reflections form a study in comparative jurisprudence; they do no more than to set some rules of the secular legal wisdom of our age side by side with an example of the traditional administration of justice in our church.

In the spirit of an academic study without prejudice, *sine ira et studio*, I shall first present our ecclesiastical procedures for handling offenses in doctrinal matters. I shall then compare them to the norms of justice and fairness as they are professed widely by modern jurisprudence and practiced in a good number of nations. By turning to a secular model in a search for proven values, I follow a venerable tradition. Paul the Apostle wrote to the Philippians: "whatever is true, whatever is honorable, whatever is just . . . think about these things . . . and the God of peace will be with you" (Phil 4:8-9). As we all know, the church considered the merits of ancient Roman law and adopted it for its own use.[2]

On the feast of Saints Peter and Paul on June 29, 1997, the Roman Congregation for the Doctrine of Faith promulgated new procedural rules titled *Regulations for the Examination of Doctrines*.[3] These have superseded the norms

---

1. See David J. O'Brien and Thomas A. Shannon, eds., *Catholic Social Thought: The Documentary Heritage* (New York: Orbis, 1995); *Compendium of the Social Doctrine of the Church* (Vatican City: Libreria Editrice Vaticana, 2004).

2. See Albert Gauthier, *Roman Law and its Contribution to Canon Law* (Ottawa: Saint Paul University, 1996).

3. AAS 89 (1997) 830–35.

published in 1971.[4] The *Explanatory Note* attached to the document and published by the same office stated: "After twenty-five years of experience . . . it was decided to prepare new *Regulations* that might respond even better to the demands of the present day."[5]

To speak of "the demands of the present day," the demands of justice, is to speak of expectations written at large in human minds and hearts. Does the document fulfill such expectations? That is the question.

THE *REGULATIONS FOR THE EXAMINATION OF DOCTRINES*

We are dealing with a short text of fifteen hundred words in the original Latin, divided into twenty-nine "articles." Its authority is that of a decree by a congregation: the pope approved it for publication but did not make its content his own, except for two articles (28 and 29) that were "specially" approved by the pope and raised to the level of pontifical law.

The wording of the title is the first clue for understanding the content of the *Regulations*: the prime focus of the examination is an affirmation or a set of assertions—a doctrine and not a person. The outcome of the process, however, will concern the proponent of the doctrine—a human person who might be held innocent or guilty.

The introductory remarks identify the principal agent in the process, the Congregation for the Doctrine of Faith. Its task is "to promote and to safeguard the doctrine of faith and morals throughout the Catholic world" (art. 1) and to see that the people of God receive the Gospel in its authenticity and integrity.

The *Regulations*[6] recall that in matters of doctrine the bishops of the particular churches also have the right and duty to exercise a pastoral solicitude both individually and collectively. The Holy See, however, has the power to intervene, and intends to intervene whenever a publication constitutes a grave danger for the faith and the impact reaches beyond the boundaries of a local episcopal conference.

To understand the role of various organs and persons referred to in the *Regulations*, it is necessary to know some basic information about the operational structures of a congregation within the Roman Curia.[7]

---

4. AAS 63 (1971) 234–36.

5. PB, art. 49.

6. In this chapter, whenever a term is used in the specific sense that it has in the *Regulations*, it is printed in italics.

7. See PB and its extensive commentary by Piero Antonio Bonnet and Carlo Gullo, eds., *La Curia Romana nella Const. Ap. "Pastor Bonus"* (Vatican City: Libreria Editrice Vaticana, 1990).

When the term *congregation* is used broadly and colloquially, it designates a department (known also as *dicastery*) with the department's personnel and offices within the administrative organization of the Holy See. When the same term is used strictly and canonically, it means a group of cardinals and bishops (exceptionally also clerics of lesser dignity but clerics only) who, as a collective body, are in charge of a department; legally they constitute the congregation. They meet either in a *plenary session* (about once a year) to which the members from the world over are invited, or in an *ordinary session* (held weekly or less frequently) where the members residing in Rome are expected to be present. A Cardinal-Archbishop-Prefect presides over each congregation; he is assisted by an Archbishop-Secretary.

A permanent staff, called the *office*, carries out the daily work of the congregation. The major administrators (Prefect, Secretary, heads of sections, etc.) form a particular council named the *congress*. Its principal task is to handle daily business and as needed prepare the cases to be examined at a forthcoming ordinary session.

As a rule, every Roman congregation relies heavily on the work of *external consultors* that the pope appoints for their expertise.

From this general description of the structures of a congregation, I turn to the presentation of the specific procedures of the Congregation for the Doctrine of Faith.

Preliminary Examination (article 3)

Is an investigation warranted?

Whenever the suspicion arises that some doctrine in circulation may be erroneous or dangerous, the office is called on (presumably by the Prefect or the Secretary) to initiate an investigation. The officials' task is to identify the writings with suspicious content, gather any relevant evidence, and submit all of them to the congress.

The congress then decides if the office should do an in-depth study.

In-Depth Study by the Office (articles 4–7)

Is a formal process needed?

The office is commissioned to study the writings under suspicion with the help of external consultors and *ad hoc experts* (as necessary) and then to report again to the congress.

The congress has several options: it can dismiss the case, it can send it for appropriate action to a local superior (bishop or religious superior), or it can order a formal process either in "ordinary" or in "urgent" form.

Examination in Ordinary Form by the Congress (articles 8–22)

Are there erroneous and/or dangerous propositions in the writings?

The process consists of two stages: the first is internal and takes place in complete secrecy, while the second is external and allows limited publicity.

First Sequence in Secrecy

The congress commissions a *council of consultors* to examine the writings in question and to ascertain if the author's doctrine does or does not conform to the church's teaching.

To help these experts, the congress appoints a *relator* for the author whose task is to represent and uphold the author's interest. He should see that the author's opinions are correctly understood and that the examiners are informed of the "positive aspects" of the author's writings.

The consultors conclude their investigation with a *formal session*. While taking into account the earlier study prepared by the office, they discuss the case. The relator for the author must be present and have a voice; the author's Ordinary (his or her diocesan bishop or religious superior) *may be* invited to participate in the debate. If so, he is bound to secrecy. Once the discussion is over, the consultors alone decide if the author's writings contain erroneous propositions and/ or dangerous opinions. The criteria for the identification of an offense are much broader than those for the denial of an article of faith. They include the Nicene Creed, subsequent solemn definitions, determinations by the ordinary magisterium, and "definitive teachings" by a pope or by the episcopal college. They may also include official pronouncements not intended to be definitive.[8]

The council's judgment with all acts and minutes are brought before the ordinary session of the Congregation. The members may decide either to drop the case or to pursue it by confronting the author with his erroneous propositions and/or dangerous opinions. Their decision, however, needs to be submitted to the *pope*.

If the pope consents to the continuing of the process, the case continues but its focus changes. Up to this point, the question was whether the writings were deficient; now the issue of the author's culpability comes into the fore. The findings speak against him. Accordingly, he is "indicted,"[9] that is, charged

---

8. See "Professio fidei et Iusiurandum fidelitatis," AAS 81 (1989) 104–6; AAS 90 (1998) 542–51; commentary by Ladislas Orsy, *The Profession of Faith and the Oath of Fidelity* (Wilmington, DE: Glazier, 1990).

9. I am borrowing from secular criminal law the terms "indicted" and "charge" to explain the process, but they must not be taken in the strict technical sense they have in secular jurisprudence.

(accused) with spreading erroneous or dangerous opinions, a crime ("delict") against the faith in canon law. The news is communicated to his Ordinary, to any other Ordinary who may have interest in the case, and to the competent departments of the Holy See (i.e., those that need to be concerned about the outcome of the investigation).

Second Sequence with Limited Publicity

Next, the Congregation informs the author, through his Ordinary, of the findings and provides him with a list of the objectionable propositions—with explanations for the negative judgments. The *Regulations* do not say who is competent to provide the explanations. At any rate, the identity of the "explainer" must not be revealed.

With the consent of his Ordinary, the author is entitled to appoint an *advisor* for himself. This advisor is not an "advocate" or an attorney in the usual sense, with the legal duty to defend the author; he is closer to a private counselor who has the right to be present at the author's side.

The author has three months to respond concerning the contested propositions. His Ordinary is encouraged to express an opinion.

The author has no right to appear before his judges, but the Congregation (presumably the Prefect) may grant permission for a dialogue between the author (with his advisor present) and the delegates of the Congregation. At the meeting, minutes must be taken and signed by all.

If the author responds, the congress is competent to receive his answer. Should it contain new grounds for reconsideration, the congress may choose to remit the case to the council of consultors. Finally, the response of the author, together with the result of the renewed consultations (if any), must be submitted to the ordinary session of the Congregation.

If the author does not respond, the same ordinary session is competent to make "an appropriate decision."

Examination in Urgent Form (articles 23–27)

How to handle an emergency?

A "process in urgency" is authorized whenever it is clear and certain that the writings of an author contain errors that are either threatening to harm the faith of the people or are already causing damage among the faithful.

The congress is competent to declare an emergency and a need for immediate action. After the declaration, it must send information to all Ordinaries who may have interest in the case and to the competent departments of the Holy See. Then it appoints a commission to precisely identify the erroneous and dangerous opinions.

The next task of the congress is to submit the harmful propositions to the ordinary session of the Congregation, which must give priority handling to the case. If its judgment is condemnatory, the decision must go to the pope for his approval.

If the pope ratifies the sentence, the author is notified and is given three months for correcting his opinions. He may request, however, permission to offer a written explanation. The ordinary session is competent to receive it and to judge it.

Sanctions (articles 28–29)

Guilty or not guilty?

If the author has not corrected his errors "in a satisfactory way and with adequate publicity" and the ordinary session has found him guilty of "the offense of heresy, apostasy, or schism, the Congregation proceeds to declare [and confirm] the *latae sententiae* [automatic] penalties [already] incurred." The reference to Canon 1364 § 1 of the Code of Canon law makes clear that the penalty is excommunication.[10] Further, the *Regulations* state, "against such a declaration no recourse is admitted." If the author has been found guilty of a lesser offense, the Congregation is entitled to impose a lesser sanction according to the general norms of the law.

Articles 28 and 29 carry the special approval of the pope; they therefore have the binding force of pontifical law.

THE LEGAL WISDOM OF OUR AGE

As I reflect on the contemporary state of secular jurisprudence—on the acceptable legal wisdom in our age—I really speak of aspirations and expectations that are partially realized, because there is no place in the world where they are fully put into practice. But there is a converging desire all over the world for justice that serves and honors the dignity of the human person. There are also serious attempts, and some remarkable successes, among the nations to create legal systems that translate the lofty ideals into binding and enforceable norms.[11]

---

10. The *Regulations* warn that if an accused does not correct his position within the time allotted to him, the Congregation may proceed to the declaration of excommunication. This may happen even if the author has never had the opportunity to explain his thoughts to his judges.

11. Throughout this chapter I avoid invoking "due process," as it is not a helpful concept for doing comparative law. The potential for misunderstandings is great. There are those who say that as long as a procedure follows the rules, it is due process, and that is the end of

In each of the following paragraphs I shall state a general principle held in honor by modern jurisprudence and meant to protect human rights. Then I shall recall the relevant content of the *Regulations* and see how far our practice fulfills the ideals of the legal wisdom of our times.

Justice demands the precise definition of an offense.

The principle speaks for itself: the less precise the definition of a misdeed, the greater the danger of injustice because a great multitude of actions can be brought under the definition. A vague term opens the door to broad accusations and restricts the scope of the defense. (Totalitarian states like to have crimes broadly defined, such as "offense against the state," "subversive speech," and so forth.)

The *Regulations* name two offenses, namely, the spreading of "erroneous doctrine" and "dangerous doctrine." Both are too broad for comfort.

"Erroneous doctrine" can have different meanings in the realm of religious beliefs and opinions. Catholic theology has always carefully distinguished revealed doctrine ("articles of faith") from theological opinions held by scholars or some church officials. They are not of the same category. If a proposition is judged erroneous, to understand the gravity of the error one must know the authority of the "truth" that it denies. Vatican Council II insisted on a "hierarchy of truths," with each truth demanding assent to a specific degree, yet the *Regulations* use one broad category that opens the door for a uniform prosecution of errors, whether major or minor. There is a difference between obstinate rejection of an article of faith and thoughtful opposition to an opinion held by an office of the Holy See.

The expression "dangerous doctrine" gives an even larger scope to the investigators: with it they can reach far and wide as it has no firm and objective limits. Dangers can be sensed in many situations. People and communities can be perceived as being exposed to dangers of different sorts. But the perception of a danger can be subjective and deceptive: much depends on the mind of the observer. I recall how many times during Vatican Council II, before the doctrine of episcopal collegiality was finally approved, its opponents, cardinals and bishops, demanded that the doctrine should be discarded because it was dangerous. Collegiality could undermine the primacy and lead to conciliarism, so they warned. Today we all hold that collegiality belongs to the core of Catholic tradition, even if we still argue about its precise definition. Many times

---

the discussion. Because the expression originates in common law jurisprudence, it is often received with fear and suspicion by lawyers educated in civil law systems; they are uncertain as to what it may cover.

in the course of Christian history, true insights emerged but uninformed people in positions of power cried "danger!" Did not the bishops of Paris and of London judge Aquinas's doctrine dangerous? Was not Galileo condemned because his theories were dangerous? To make ill-defined or undefined danger a juridical ground for condemnation is to endanger the operation of justice.

Justice is best served when the respective roles of the judge, the prosecutor, and the defendant's advocate are kept separate.

The aim of any judicial process is to help the judge(s) arrive at an impartial and detached judgment. Accumulated experience of courts and tribunals, beginning with the practice of the ancient Greeks and Romans, has shown that when the roles are fused, justice is in jeopardy. The reason lies in the limitations of our human nature. The dynamics of the investigation and of the trial carry the specialized participants in opposite directions, and rightly so. If the office of the investigator appoints all of them, the balance of the trial is disturbed and the objectivity of the decision may be questioned.[12]

In the *Regulations*, this well-established separation of the roles is not honored. The same organs of the Congregation are involved in, or can have influence on the initial investigation, the articulation of the charges, the defense of the writings and of the author, and eventually the final decision.

Even if we assume that in ideal circumstances justice could be done, a question still remains: "Would we see that justice had been done?"

Equity, the perfection of justice, demands that each of the opposing parties has a similar opportunity to plead before the judge.

Any trial is a dialectical exchange of arguments among the participants. The exchange is meant to help the judge and all involved to obtain reasonable knowledge of all relevant rules and facts. In this exercise, justice demands fair play, similar opportunity for both sides. If one of the parties does not receive as thorough an opportunity to speak and to be heard as the other party, the procedure is vitiated.

The *Regulations* grant different measures, far from any equal amount of time, to the accuser and the defender. During the first part of the ordinary process when the crucial decision is taken about the conformity of the author's writings to the demands of orthodoxy, he is absent. He is not even informed that a

---

12. The oddity of a rule that requires the investigator to appoint the defender is better realized if we hypothetically reverse the roles: what would happen if in a criminal trial the defense team had the right to appoint the prosecutor!

process has been initiated. True, the investigators must appoint a relator to defend the author, but is there not a conflict of interest? Besides, what is the guarantee that this relator understands the author?

Another glaring lack of equity (to say the least) emerges when the outcome of the examination is negative, and the Congregation finds the author's propositions "erroneous or dangerous." By rule, and from a position of high authority, the Congregation must inform the author's Ordinary and the competent offices of the Holy See. Inevitably, such communication would tarnish, if not destroy, the author's reputation. It would certainly mark him—at home and in high places—as suspect and not to be trusted. While this communication is circulating, the author might still be in a state of total ignorance as to what is happening, with no opportunity to explain or defend himself.

Yet, equity and fairness—justice—would demand that before any publicity takes place, the author should be given the opportunity to explain his own writings to the examiners who may not be familiar with them and may even lack the necessary cultural and linguistic background to understand them correctly. The risk, therefore, of a serious misunderstanding is ever present and always high. For a historical precedent, we should recall how much misunderstanding that degenerated into mistrust arose between the Greeks and the Latins, and, also, how erroneous and adversary assumptions contributed to the separation of the churches.

Our church has nothing to lose and much to gain by offering the elementary courtesy to Christian thinkers to explain their mind right from the moment when suspicion arises against their writings. It may even happen that by allowing an initial clarification, the investigation may turn into a learning process for the benefit of the officials in charge of the case.

The judges have the duty to presume the accused innocent and protect him until the evidence proves beyond a reasonable doubt that he is guilty and to enforce the rule that the burden of proof is on the accuser.

The "principle of the presumption of innocence" is an inviolable part of the criminal proceedings in modern legal systems. Such a presumption, however, is not mentioned in the *Regulations.* Yet the rule should operate right from the beginning of the process, even in the examination of the writings. We have a classical text, and wise caution, in the beginning of the *Book of the Spiritual Exercises* by Ignatius of Loyola:

> It should be presupposed that every good Christian ought to be more eager to put a good interpretation on a neighbor's statement than to condemn it. Further, if one cannot interpret it favorably, one should ask how the other means it. If

that meaning is wrong, one should correct the other person with love; and if this is not enough, one should search out every appropriate means through which, by understanding the statement in a good way, it may be saved. (22)

Sapienti sat: for the wise no more needs to be said.

The problem of the proper role of the prosecution arises again and in a crucial way when the Congregation's conclusion concerning the writings is negative and its officials must confront the author with the propositions that they have already judged erroneous and/or dangerous. It must be a difficult task for anyone who pronounced a "guilty" sentence over the *writings* of a person to be a detached judge when deciding the innocence or guilt of the same *person.*

No good reason exists why within the Congregation a system could not be set by which the judges remain distinct in every way from the examiners and the accusers. After all, the Code of Canon Law prescribes that in a diocesan tribunal, for example, there should be judges and a "promoter of justice," whose task is similar to that of the examiners. *There,* it is unthinkable to have the same persons perform the different tasks. If it ever happened, the sentence would be irreparably null and void. A good reason exists for the Congregation to follow the same method.

Justice demands openness.

The virtue of justice, as integrated with faith, hope, and love among Christians, is a powerful factor in forging unity in the community. For this reason, it is never enough to do justice, it must be done publicly. The people should see that justice is done.

Of course, prudence and discretion may require some confidentiality. When it is needed, so be it. But when there are no greater values in jeopardy, openness should be the rule. A trial is never about one single individual: the accused is a member of a community of believers. Whether he is guilty or not, the community nurtured him and suffers with him. It is fair, therefore, that the community should be informed in a prudent manner. Transparency does not mean unbridled publicity; there are many ways of communicating among responsible people.

Overall, the *Regulations* fall short of the standards of an open trial. In particular, the first part of the ordinary proceedings is shrouded in complete secrecy.

The opportunity for appeal is an integral part of any good judicial system.

To leave room for appeal is to acknowledge our human condition: we are fallible human beings, judges included. A judicial process with no possibility of appeal is a scary system for anyone to contemplate, for it leaves no room for the correction of mistakes. It amounts to attributing a sort of infallibility to human judges, who have never been promised exceptional divine assistance.

The *Regulations* are clear: once the Congregation has declared that the author is guilty of heresy, apostasy, or schism, the author must be held excommunicated, and "against such a declaration no recourse is admitted" (art. 28). The *Explanatory Notes* provide the following reason: throughout the process the pope himself is involved; hence, there *cannot* be any room for appeal. The underlying assumption seems to be that throughout, papal infallibility somehow plays a part in the process and, at the end, seals the sentence. But Catholic theology allows no such assumption. To exclude, therefore, any possibility of a miscarriage of justice would be presumptuous.

At this point the *Regulations* reveal a substantial structural weakness: they create a first instance tribunal that, in the course of the *same trial*, becomes a supreme court. Interestingly, in marriage cases the Roman Rota admits appeals even against its own decisions. How much more prudent it would be to admit an appeal in a doctrinal case!

Most unusually, the *Regulations* signal that the papal office is (must be?) involved at various stages of the trial. As a result of this, no appeal can be admitted. Logically, it should follow that if a miscarriage of justice occurs, the blame must be on the successor of Peter—not a good prospect for any faithful person to contemplate.

Remarks about the penalty of automatic excommunication.

Excommunication is an extreme penalty in a Christian community. The bond of baptism remains; however, he or she is denied nourishment, a member of the body is paralyzed. As with all extreme penalties, it hurts both the individual and the whole group. The person is spiritually incapacitated, for he or she cannot receive the sacraments. The social body suffers the trauma of an amputation; its "wholeness" is diminished.[13]

---

13. The *Regulations* warn that if an accused does not correct his position within the time allotted to him, the Congregation may proceed to the declaration of excommunication. This may happen even if the author has never had the opportunity to explain his thoughts to his judges.

The *Regulations* ignore a crucial problem: the crime of heresy is an "obstinate denial" of an article of faith (Canon 751); it is surrender to falsehood while one sees the light. Such a self-destructing act is certainly no less possible than suicide is possible, but it is not an ordinary event. Even if it has been established that the writings of a person contain heretical propositions, it does not follow necessarily that he is guided by a perverse intention. To rush into the imposition of an extreme sentence (perhaps without ever having listened to the author) can hardly be the sign and symbol of justice—let alone Christian mercy. Most of the

The so-called *latae sententiae,* "automatic," excommunication should be understood for what it is: an anachronism that hurts modern sensitivities with its inhumanity. The offender is mandated to be his own accuser, judge, and executioner—a near-impossible task.[14]

Many thoughtful theologians and canonists suggested before the last revision of the Code of Canon Law that automatic excommunications (referred to as "legion") should be abolished altogether. The reviewers listened and abolished many, but in the end they retained a few. To delete them all from canon law would be no loss to the faithful or to the reputation of the church.

In a more general way, no one can tell if excommunications have done more good than harm to the church in the course of its history. But we know that some excommunications have caused long-lasting harm. We recall the hasty and tragic gesture of Humbert, the papal legate in Constantinople who in 1054 excommunicated the Patriarch and thus contributed to the enduring severance of the two sister churches. We may ponder the impact of the excommunication of Elizabeth I by Pius V in 1570, a sentence that effectively destroyed any hope of reconciliation between the English monarchy and the See of Rome.

Finally, a story unfolding in our days should cause us to pause. There is an increasing consensus among theologians and historians that on some counts the Council of Trent misunderstood the teachings of the Reformers and consequently several of its *anathemata* were misplaced.[15] Ecumenical scholars are putting immense effort into the disentangling of such misperceptions. Probably much harm (and violence) could have been avoided had the opposing parties made a greater effort to understand each other. We have a cautionary tale for today: if such calamity could have occurred around an ecumenical council, they could surely occur at an ecclesiastical court.

CONCLUSION

A conclusion emerges in stark simplicity: for anyone educated in the sensitivities of modern jurisprudence, the *Regulations* do not respond, as they

---

time, for the good of the community it should be enough to state with authority what our Catholic doctrine is and what our tradition is not and then let time, fraternal correction, and divine grace have their gentle impact on the author.

14. *Latae sententiae* excommunications may have made better sense in ancient times when criminals were beyond the reach of ordinary justice because of the immense distances and the lack of communications. Today a wrongdoer can be more easily identified and named whenever the well-being of the community demands a punitive action.

15. It may have happened that while the condemnation of an error was correct, the attribution of that error to an individual was incorrect; Origen certainly did not fall into all the errors attributed to him by his enemies.

were intended, to the demands of the present day. They are hardly signs or symbols of justice for our age. They have their roots in past ages; they were not born from the vision of human dignity and the respect for honest conscience that is demanded the world over today.

The integral mission of the Congregation goes well beyond investigating, prosecuting, and punishing offenses against the faith. It embraces "promoting and safeguarding [the] doctrine of faith and morals throughout the Catholic world."[16] The *Regulations* are not in harmony with such a mission.

In the Catholic world, the best way to promote and safeguard the doctrine of faith is to create a climate of trust where the process described by St. Anselm of Canterbury as *fides quaerens intellectum*, "faith seeking understanding," can flourish. Such a search for understanding is carried out mostly (but not exclusively) by professional theologians. To attract young and talented persons to choose theological research and reflection as their vocation, to strengthen those who are already dedicated to that work, and to lift the spirit of those who are struggling with the hard issues of our days, an environment of freedom and confidence is indispensable, a *condicio sine qua non*. Such an environment cannot exist if investigations, accusations, and even condemnations are allowed to take place in secrecy.

Creative thinkers who scrutinize the divine mysteries and give us a language to speak about them must be constantly aware that the church trusts them and protects them. If norms are needed to prevent deviations, norms are even more necessary to secure freedom for creative thinking.

In truth, creative thinkers are one of the greatest assets of the church: they let the internal riches of the evangelical message unfold. As our world evolves, new questions are continually raised about the content and understanding of the revelation, the role of religion in the political society, justice in the distribution of the resources of the earth, issues of morality, and so forth—who can name them all? Learned persons who are capable of reaching new insights into our old tradition can be of valuable (even indispensable) assistance to the hierarchy, which has the final judgment in doctrinal matters, and to all the faithful who are seeking the intelligence of the mysteries with a sincere heart. This was the ministry of Friar Thomas Aquinas and of Cardinal John Henry Newman.

The judicial procedures of the *Regulations* are of human origin. They are not rooted in any divine precept. They are the product of another age, not suited for our ecumenical times. To reform such procedures would be to obey Vatican Council II: "Christ summons the church, as she goes her pilgrim way, to that

16. PB, art. 48.

continual reformation of which she always has need, insofar as she is a human institution here on earth" (UR 6).

Ultimately, we should trust the internal strength of the Word of God. Cardinal Newman's insight in chapter 8 of his *Essay on the Development of Christian Doctrine* remains as valid today as ever: "The stronger and more living an idea [is], that is, the more powerful hold it exercises on the minds of men, the more able it [is] to dispense with safeguards, and trust to itself against the danger of corruption."

There is no stronger "idea" given to the human race than the idea of Christianity. The source of its "internal vigor" (Newman's words) is the living Spirit of God.

8

Stability and Development in Canon Law
The Case of Definitive Doctrine

The beginning of knowledge is wonder, wonder provoked by a puzzle whose pieces do not seem to fit together. We do have such an ongoing puzzle in canon law; it is the prima facie conflict between the demand of stability and the imperative of development.

Stability is an essential quality of any good legal system because a community's laws are an expression of its identity, and there is no identity without permanency. Many times we hear in the United States that we are a country held together by our laws. Although the statement cannot be the full truth, it is obvious that if our laws ever lost their stability, the nation's identity would be imperiled. In a religious community where the source of its identity is in the common memory of a divine revelation, the demand for stability is even stronger. Fidelity to the "Word of God" becomes the principal virtue.

Yet, any good legal system must be open and receptive to developments. No community, secular or religious, can be frozen in time and live. Absolute stillness means death. In a political community, the internal energies of the citizenry and the pressing forces of history have their unrelenting impact on the laws and demand changes. Similar forces operate in a religious community: the "gathering" of the believers, *ecclesia*, is never a static monument. It is a living body animated by internal resources and responding to external influences. The eschatological destiny of the members (their expectation of eternal life) does not protect them from the vicissitudes of history.

Thus, the demand for stability and the imperative of development are vital forces in any living community; they operate in both nations and churches. The question, therefore, is not how the one could be eliminated and the other kept. Nor could it be which of the two should prevail. Both are needed. Our inquiry can be only about their respective roles and a desirable balance between the two that protects the group's identity and leaves enough space for the imperative of growth and expansion.

Stability in the world of the laws creates a sense of security in the subjects. Legal developments offer them increasing opportunities to use their potential.

Catholic believers see the church as well grounded in stability: Christ is its founder, his Spirit its life-giver. No one can take away the memory of the evangelical message and no one can strangle the forces of divine energy. The same believers, however, often perceive development as problematic: "How can we know," they ask, "true progress from deceptive change? How can we differentiate healthy growth from sickly decline?"

A seasoned answer is available: it comes from Cardinal John Henry Newman. In his *Essay on the Development of Christian Doctrine*, published in its final form in 1878, Newman proposed a theory that is as valid today as it was in his day.[1] His interest was primarily in explaining the development of doctrine in the Christian church, but most of what he said is applicable to the development of canon law.

He proposed seven positive criteria for recognizing genuine developments and as many negative marks for identifying destructive changes. For brevity's sake, I pull them together and summarize them under three headings.

The positive signs are the following: First, a healthy development respects the foundations of the institution—its identity remains intact, and the leading principles of its existence and operations are not destroyed. Second, true development shows a harmonious progress from the old to the new—it is the fruit of historical continuity, the roots of the new are in the old, and the once-hidden potentials of the old are revealed in the new. Third, the new has vigor of life—it is filled with energy, and it brings life to its surroundings.

These signs speak even more clearly if we contrast them with their opposites, the signs of decline: First, a false development destabilizes the foundations of an institution—it has a corrosive impact on the community's identity, and it undermines the original principles of its activities. Second, in the transition from the old to the new there is a radical break—the new does not grow out of the old, and the image of the old cannot be found in the new. Third, the new shows no vigor of life, it exhibits decay—it weakens the institution, and it leads to stagnation, alienation, and loss of quality of life.

Now we have workable criteria by which to judge what is, or what is not, an authentic development in the realm of doctrine and in the realm of law.

---

1. The book had many editions and reprints; for an edition with extensive critical apparatus, see John Henry Newman, *An Essay on the Development of Christian Doctrine*, ed. Charles Harrold (Longmans, Green and Co., 1949). In particular, see chap. 5, "Genuine Developments Contrasted with Corruptions," pp. 55–91.

THE CASE OF DEFINITIVE TEACHING

By way of introducing the case of "definitive teaching," let me state firmly that in matters of doctrine stability is essential. The faithful must not lose the memory of the evangelical message; it is the source of their identity. Yet, as a seed must be sown, then strike roots, and grow into a plant, the message sown in the mind and heart of the people must strike roots, grow, and produce fruit that is the intelligence of faith. Such development is equally essential for the evangelical message—sown by Christ. Vatican Council II expressed this balance well:

> The universal body of the faithful who have received the anointing of the holy one . . . cannot be mistaken in belief. . . . It adheres indefectibly to "the faith which was once for all delivered to the saints" (Jude 3); it penetrates more deeply into that same faith through right judgment and applies it more fully to life. (LG 12)

"It adheres indefectibly": there is the demand of stability. "It penetrates more deeply": there is the imperative of development.

An oft-quoted traditional rule expresses well the ideal balance between stability and development in matters of belief, "in necessary things unity, in doubtful things liberty, in all things charity." The "necessary things" are what we need to believe because they belong to the very core of the Christian Tradition; we must be one in professing them.[2] In modern, mainly post–Vatican I, times such doctrines are often described as "articles of faith infallibly taught." They are articulated in our creeds, in the "determinations" of the ecumenical councils, and in the papal "definitions." They are also proclaimed in the daily worship of the universal church.

The "doubtful things" are not teachings that Christians ought to doubt or contest but points of doctrine that, as yet, have not been fully authenticated in any of the legitimate ways as integral parts of the Tradition.[3] They are positions and opinions (usually inherited) that ought to be respected but are in need of scrutiny to discover their full significance for the community. For such an inquiry liberty is essential.

Charity, of course, needs no explanation.

---

2. In Christian theology it is customary to distinguish between Tradition (with a capital *T*) and traditions. The former refers to the one and undivided core of the evangelical message that must be kept intact. The latter refers to historical accretions that may be venerable but not indispensable.

3. Such legitimate ways include, for example, the whole church so believing, ecumenical councils so teaching, popes so defining.

THE CODE OF CANON LAW—1983

The Code of Canon Law, promulgated in 1983, mandated a healthy balance between stability and development. Its Canon 750 stressed the importance of stability:

> A person must believe with divine and Catholic faith all those things contained in the word of God, written or handed on, that is, in the one deposit of faith entrusted to the Church, and at the same time proposed as divinely revealed either by the solemn magisterium of the Church or by its ordinary and universal magisterium which is manifested by the common adherence of the Christian faithful under the leadership of the sacred magisterium; therefore all are bound to avoid any doctrines whatsoever contrary to them.

Canon 218 asserted the imperative of development and the need for "just freedom" in research:

> Those engaged in the sacred disciplines have a just freedom of inquiry and of expressing their opinion prudently on those matters in which they possess expertise, while observing the submission due to the magisterium of the Church.

The two canons together stated well the right and duty of the community—to preserve and to let evolve the evangelical doctrine. In case of conflict between the two tasks, an additional norm tipped the scale in the favor of development, as Canon 749 § 3 prescribed: "No doctrine is understood as defined infallibly unless this is manifestly evident." In other words, the researcher must be free to investigate and report on his findings unless it is manifest that he would undermine infallible teaching. In legal language, there is a presumption in favor of the "faith seeking understanding."[4]

THE APOSTOLIC LETTER "*MOTU PROPRIO*"—1998

This balance established by the Code of Canon Law, however, was changed in 1998 with the promulgation of the *Motu Proprio Ad tuendam fidem*.[5] The letter introduced into, and imposed on, the church a new category of teaching, called "definitive," and explained it as not infallible but irreformable. Effectively, if not verbally, it transferred some freely debated doctrines from the field of the "doubtful things" to the field of the "necessary things," where no question

---

4. The church can afford such generosity. After all, the Spirit is protecting its collective memory.

5. AAS 90 (1998) 457–61.

must be raised anymore about their unchangeable nature.[6] To this effect, the *Motu Proprio* added a second paragraph to Canon 750 (the original text has become paragraph one). The added text reads:

> Each and every thing which is proposed definitively by the magisterium of the Church concerning the doctrine of faith and morals, that is, each and every thing which is required to safeguard reverently and to expound faithfully the same deposit of faith, is also to be firmly embraced and retained; therefore, one who refuses those propositions which are to be held definitively is opposed to the doctrine of the Catholic Church.

Thus the document places each and every point of teaching that has been declared "definitive" by the papal magisterium into the body of "the doctrine of the Catholic Church," even when such a declaration does not fulfill the stringent criteria of a papal definition—criteria that Vatican Council I articulated with meticulous care after much search and fierce debate.

> The Roman Pontiff, when he speaks ex cathedra, that is, when, acting in the office of shepherd and teacher of all Christians, he defines, by virtue of his supreme apostolic authority, a doctrine concerning faith and morals to be held by the universal church, possesses through the divine assistance promised to him in the person of blessed Peter, the infallibility with which the divine Redeemer willed his church to be endowed.[7]

Vatican Council II confirmed this definition and articulated its limit with some precision: "This infallibility . . . extends just as far as the deposit of divine revelation that is to be guarded as sacred and faithfully expounded" (LG 25).

In protecting the stability of doctrine, the Apostolic Letter went beyond the "deposit of revelation" when it declared that "each and everything [doctrine] which is required to safeguard reverently and expound faithfully the same deposit of faith" can be the object of a definitive statement and thus must

---

6. The "Commentary" added to the *Motu Proprio* and signed by the Prefect and the Secretary of the Congregation for the Doctrine of Faith but not approved by the Congregation as a corporate body (hence having no official standing) gives some examples of "definitive" teachings. For example, it lists the reservation of priestly ordination only to men, the illicitness of euthanasia, the illicitness of prostitution, the legitimacy of the election of the pope, the validity of an ecumenical council, the canonization of saints, and the invalidity of Anglican orders. The list seems to intend to bring (not conceptually but practically) under papal infallibility a good number of sundry points of doctrines that many theologians considered disputed questions. It is difficult to determine what the common criterion was for the selection for the doctrines listed.

7. "First Dogmatic Constitution on the Church of Christ" (*Pastor aeternus*), in *The Christian Faith*, ed. Jacques Dupuis (New York: Alba House, 1990) 298. For the original Latin see DS 3074.

be embraced and held as irreformable. Several commentators noted that, with the help of the theory of "definitive teaching," papal infallibility has been expanded beyond the constitutions of Vatican I and II and beyond the limits "canonized" by the Council.

To enforce the observance of this new provision, the *Motu Proprio* added a clause to Canon 1371, 1°, that institutes "just penalty" for anyone who fails to embrace and hold all and each that are definitively proposed and "obstinately rejects the doctrine mentioned in Canon 750 § 2 or in Canon 752, and who does not retract after having been admonished by the Apostolic See or an ordinary." Such persons, although not heretics, are "opposed to the doctrine of the Catholic Church" (Canon 750 § 2).

AN ASSESSMENT

What is the result of this new legislation? It has created a new balance between stability and development. In the practical order, it has increased—as no law has ever done it before—the "necessary things," the doctrines that must be held, and it has decreased the "doubtful things," teachings that were disputed questions. It has done so not merely by normative directions but also by punitive sanctions. This was a break with the explicit policy of Vatican Council II, which wanted to proclaim the good news but refused to bolster its teaching with the threat of criminal actions.[8] Also to be noted is that the sanction in a given case can be heavy, since the delict is being "opposed to the doctrine of the Catholic Church," which is, presumably, just one notch under the crime of heresy.

The scope of Canon 218's affirming freedom in research is now more narrowly drawn. Canon 749, paragraph 3, stating that nothing should be held infallible unless it is manifestly so proven, has become moot because some doctrines must be held irreformable even if they are not infallible, and persons in no way contesting infallible doctrine may be punished for being "opposed to the doctrine of the Catholic Church."[9]

All this is canon law now. The universal church has the task of receiving it, not in the sense of legal ratification but in the sense of understanding it and

---

8. It is noteworthy that the opening paragraph of the Apostolic Letter strikes a note of distrust: "To protect the Catholic faith against errors arising on the part of some of the Christian faithful, in particular among those who studiously dedicate themselves to the discipline of sacred theology, it appeared highly necessary . . . to add new norms." I know no precedent in the acts of the Holy See for such a sweeping indictment of the Catholic theologians.

9. Looking into the future, one can anticipate that much ink will flow (or many printouts will be produced) dealing with the question of how a proposition that is not guaranteed to be infallible can remain forever irreformable.

assimilating its content. Such a reception is bound to be a complex and long, drawn-out process.

To reject the legislation would not be a Catholic response. Since it comes from an authoritative source, it must be received with *obsequium*, respect, in the canonical language.[10] Canon 752 is applicable:

> Although not an assent of faith, a religious submission [*obsequium*, respect, loyalty] of the intellect and will must be given to a doctrine which the Supreme Pontiff or the college of bishops declares concerning faith or morals when they exercise the authentic magisterium . . .

Obsequium, however, cannot determine the doctrinal weight of a document. That is a matter for critical theological judgment. Nor can reverence assess the degree of prudence that prompted the new legislation, for such a judgment can be articulated only from a historical distance.

While this process of reception is getting under way, some comments are in order.

The initial question for any commentator needs to be about the weight of authority behind the Apostolic Letter. By way of exclusion, the letter does not carry the authenticating marks of infallibility as they were determined by Vatican Council I and confirmed by Vatican Council II, because it is not a solemn *ex cathedra* pronouncement.[11] It is a papal document of high authority,

10. The Latin term *obsequium*, as it is used in canon law, has no precise equivalent in English. "Loyalty" would be the closest to it. It has an affinity with the Italian *ossequio*, which encompasses a whole gamut of meanings, from greeting a friend with respect to paying obedience to God. In canon law its exact meaning can be conjectured from the context only. The official translation by the Canon Law Society of America renders *obsequium* with "submission," which is an interpretation, and not always the correct one. If the drafters of the Code of Canon Law had meant "submission," they had at their disposal precise Latin words such as *submissio* or *oboedientia*.

11. The pope uses his full apostolic authority when he defines, *ex cathedra*, an article of faith; it is a rare event, having happened only twice in recent history: in 1854 Pius IX defined the dogma of the Immaculate Conception, and in 1950 Pius XII proclaimed the dogma of the Assumption. The pope uses his apostolic authority, but not to its fullness, in all of his other pronouncements, such as in Apostolic Constitutions, *Motu Proprio(s)*, encyclicals, and so forth. To determine the exact weight of such teachings is always a complex task; much depends on the pope's intention (often to be reconstructed), on the internal content of the document, and on the document's historical circumstances. There cannot be any doubt that Vatican Council II more than once corrected the non-infallible teachings of recent popes. For example, it did so in matters of religious freedom, salvation outside the church, the historicity of the Scriptures, and so forth. One can ask (but no one can answer) what position a future ecumenical council would take concerning the theory of "definitive teaching." Be that as it may, Vatican Council II left no doubt that the magisterium of an ecumenical council can abandon, supersede, or modify earlier papal teachings which were not *ex cathedra* definitions. Since this happened, theologians

but not of the highest. Through this *Motu Proprio,* the theory of "definitive teaching" has entered the realm of theology, although not with the same force as the definition of infallibility did at Vatican Council I. No theologian can ignore or bypass it. Indeed, to understand its full meaning, studies are already well under way and progressing.[12]

As regards the content of the document and the substance of the issue, it is probably wise, at this point in time, for a commentator not to go beyond some tentative assessment based on Newman's criteria for authentic development. We are already in a position to raise some good questions and see where they lead us, but not in a situation to articulate well-grounded conclusions.

(1) Does the new legislation confirm the old foundations and promote the vital operations of the institution? The document certainly intends to protect the stability of the doctrinal foundations, but it seems to extend them beyond the traditional limits. It attributes unchangeable permanency to doctrines to which the universal church has not committed itself infallibly.

(2) Is the new legislation organically rooted in the old? At the very core of the new legislation is the idea of non-infallible but unchangeable teaching. It is difficult to locate the origins of the idea in the Tradition; it has appeared in the last decades only. Neither Vatican I nor Vatican II discussed definitive but non-infallible teaching to any length or in any depth. Nor has there been, as far as we know, previous to the promulgation of the *Motu Proprio* any sustained consultation on this issue among the bishops.

---

and canon lawyers must face a delicate question: In assessing the authority, and interpreting the content, of the contemporary documents of the Holy See, how far should one take into account the fact that Vatican Council II, presided over by the then-reigning popes, John XXIII and Paul VI, overruled earlier papal pronouncements of high but not of the highest authority?

12. See Symposium *Disciplinare la verita?* "Cristianesimo nella Storia" 21 (2000) (a special issue of the journal entirely dedicated to the issues raised by *Ad tuendam fidem*). This text contains the papers of an international group of theologians gathered for a symposium at the Institute of Religious Studies in Bologna, Italy. The title of the collection points to the crux of the problem of the new legislation: *Disciplinare la verita?* That is, "To discipline the truth?"

A further remark (not from Bologna) on the issue of "disciplining the truth": today, it is commonly admitted that the radical misjudgment of the Inquisition was that the truth can be imposed by force. Questions: Is it prudent to impose "definitive" doctrines with the threat of canonical penalties that in a given case can amount to the loss of authority, office, function, right, privilege, faculty, title, or insignia, even merely honorary, and so forth (Canon 1336 § 1), all at the discretion of a competent ecclesiastical superior? Does the church really need such sanctions to uphold its teaching? Does such legislation create a better environment for receiving God's gifts, which is the main purpose of canon law?

(3) Does the new legislation bring a new vigor of life to the church? The new legislation is not likely to bring new vigor into theological research. Authoritative "definitive" proclamations are bound to hamper the natural and organic evolution of the "intelligence of faith"; the community endowed by Christ with a supernatural instinct of faith cannot play its part in the discovery of truth. Perhaps even more important (tragically?), the expanding of the "irreformable" doctrines would slow down the ecumenical movement, a movement that we believe is wanted by God and sustained by God's Spirit. Sooner or later the Catholic Church must state with no ambiguity whether or not the acceptance of "definitive teachings" will be considered an absolute condition for its reunion with other Christian churches. Are we creating new obstacles?

Assessments of greater weight and of more lasting value will come over a longer period of time and from better sources than these considerations. They will come from the living church, from all and each part of it: the faithful, the episcopate, and the theologians. They, God's people, "cannot be mistaken in belief"—as Vatican Council II states. Throughout this process of "faith seeking understanding," the magisterium must be present in several ways: first by listening to the people and encouraging their efforts and then as the legitimate authority to pronounce decisive judgments.

CONCLUSION

One need not be a Hegelian to assert that, in the history of the human family, progress often comes through dialectical movements. A dominant trend is followed by its opposite, and out of their encounter, a new synthesis emerges. Such a pattern may have something to do with our human nature—we cannot comprehend the fullness of reality all at once, because we approach our complex challenges one-sidedly. Then we realize that the truth is richer than our understanding of it and we look at the other side and discover a synthesis.

This pattern of history, or this habit of the human mind, operates in the life of the church as well. There, too, we find a succession of dialectical forces. To find it, it is enough to reflect on the events of the last century. The beginnings of it were marked by strong trends in support of the stability of doctrine and institutions: the "combat" against modernism and the promulgation of the first Code of Canon Law in 1917 are good examples of it. At the end of the pontificate of Pius XII, the church lived and operated under a strong central administration. The pope was the supreme teacher and, by and large the world over, the people lived under a strict discipline, imposed and upheld by clear laws and sanctions (not to mention the far-reaching eternal punishments detailed by many moral theologians and tacitly supported by the hierarchy). Many times we heard that no ecumenical council will ever be needed again: the papacy can take care of the church. Obedience was the principal virtue.

Then came John XXIII, who in 1959, on the feast of the conversion of Saul the Persecutor who became Paul the Apostle, announced his intention to convoke an ecumenical council. With a few quiet words he reversed the forces of history. Returning to the ancient custom of the church, he wanted to listen to the bishops and invited them to speak freely—to him and to each other. He risked a new balance between stability and development, and he succeeded. At Vatican Council II creativity dominated—with no loss of stability. Not surprisingly, Cardinal John Henry Newman's ideas about development inspired many of the Council's debates.

Through the awareness of the dialectics of history, we can come to a better understanding of the church's history. Today, stability seems to be favored over creativity. Yet, in the universal body of the faithful—in the whole people—there is an immense reserve of energy; an energy that is latent, maybe, but pressing. Sooner or later, its forces are bound to break to the surface, and creative insights will abound again and surprise the observers. This seems to be the pattern of history. Or, is this the pattern that God uses to lead his people?

9

Definitive Doctrine and Ordinances Supporting It

Debating the Issues

INTRODUCTORY NOTE

In the Western church we have a venerable tradition of disciplined and respectful debates. They were initiated by Abelard through his method of *sic et non* (yes and no), then refined by the great scholastics. Such exchanges contributed mightily to a controlled development of doctrine. The *Summa Theologiae* or the *Summa contra Gentiles* of Aquinas, with the delicate play of statements such as *Videtur quod* (It seems that . . .) and *Sed contra est* (. . . on the contrary) and *Respondeo dicendum quod* (In response, it must be said that . . .), are demonstrations of skill in marshalling arguments.

A debate is nothing else than the public examination of an insight in the crucible of probing questions; it is an open effort to establish the truth.

Should we ever lose the taste for debate, we would lose much: it keeps the spirit of community alive. The exercise begins with a question, and a question is an invitation for communication. It continues with a response, and through it a bond is created between the two sides.

On May 18, 1988, John Paul II published the *Motu Proprio* titled *Ad tuendam fidem*, "To protect the faith"—a document of papal authority. It came with a *Commentary* attached to it, which was signed by the Prefect of the Congregation of the Doctrine of Faith and its Secretary—a document not of papal authority.

Concerning these two documents, especially their respective binding force and content, I published some brief observations in *Stimmen der Zeit*, a monthly journal of religion and culture published in Munich, Germany.[1]

Soon after, Cardinal Joseph Ratzinger (later Pope Benedict XVI) responded in an article in the same review, and a debate ensued. He clearly wished to

---

1. I am grateful to Martin Maier, editor of *Stimmen der Zeit*, for opening the journal to this debate and for his help and guidance throughout the exchanges.

participate in the discussions as a theologian. (Throughout the exchanges he never used the letterhead of the Congregation.) Surely, his contribution had a special significance then and there since the relevant documents were within the scope of his office. Once, however, he was elected pope, his earlier sayings and writings took on a new dimension. His earlier statements may have been the portents of future pontifical policy.

The exchanges reproduced here in English are well known in Germany; it is fair that they should be made available in English-speaking countries.

A.

Article by Ladislas Orsy,
published in Stimmen der Zeit *216 (1998) 735–40*
[English by the author]

The Authority of Ecclesiastical Documents
[Von der Autorität kirchlicher Dokumente]

Whenever the church issues a new document, the first step toward its correct understanding is to locate it in its historical context and to define its authority. On such initial assessments the correct perception of its message will depend.

In determining the document's authority, two excesses must be avoided since both are enemies of the truth. One is to downgrade it; this would happen if an interpreter tried to reduce the binding force of an apostolic constitution to that of an encouraging exhortation. Another is to upgrade it; this would occur if a commentator claimed that a statement by a church official in his personal capacity was a proclamation binding the whole faith community.

The right approach, the only way to truth, flows from intelligent fidelity. We ought to be one with the church in its firm possession of the revelation—as we must be one with the same church in its search for a better understanding of the mysteries. In each, in the downgrading and in the upgrading of authority, there is a failure in fidelity.

Much has been published, and in a short time, on the Apostolic Letter *Ad tuendam fidem* and the *Commentary* attached to it. The two are different; they come from distinct sources and are of disparate nature. The former is a piece of legislation promulgated by the pope; the latter is a personal statement signed by Cardinal Ratzinger, the Prefect of the Congregation for the Doctrine of Faith, and Archbishop Bertone, its Secretary. Theologians and reporters on religion have put more effort into explaining the documents' content than into determining their historical context and defining their degree of authority. Because of these omissions, some finer points concerning their background and binding force remain in need of further clarification. Such points are: *the insertion of new canons into the Code of Canon Law, the meaning of definitive teaching, the authority of the* Commentary, *and the issue of the expanded profession of faith.*

The New Canons. The reason given in the Apostolic Letter for the insertion of the new canons into the Code of Canon Law is that there was a *lacuna*, a gap, among the canons: the drafters had not included any specific rule concerning the acceptance of doctrine "definitively" proposed by the church. In fairness to the experts who drafted the Code, learned persons as they were, it needs to be said that they could not have perceived a *lacuna* in such matters because the category of propositions "definitively" taught, as it appears now in official documents, did not exist. A historically correct statement should be: "as the idea of definitive teaching evolved in the documents of the Holy See, the need for new canons emerged."

The new canons imposing sanctions for the rejection of definitive teaching do not really expand our criminal law. All the violations that fall under the new sanctions could have been prosecuted under the *Regulations for the Examination of Doctrines* promulgated in 1997 by the Congregation for the Doctrine of Faith. What the new canons do is to give a more exact base for such prosecution: they are forceful reminders that offenses will be punished.

At some later age, a church historian will probably point out how much the "signs of the times" have changed from the years of Vatican Council II to the end of this century. The Fathers of the Council wanted no threats or punishments in their documents; they trusted that faith will attract by its own beauty and persuasive power. As it happens now, the first reform of the present Code of Canon Law includes precisely that, threat and punishment.

Yet notwithstanding this negative aspect of the change, the initiative itself of inserting new norms into the Code has a positive dimension. It can be a precedent for a healthy process. The rigid unity of the canons has been broken, and the principle of updating the Code to developing doctrine has been introduced—the first time since 1983, the year of the promulgation of the new Code. It is right and just that as the church progresses in the understanding of doctrine its laws should be adjusted accordingly. Since the Council, we have advanced greatly in the intelligence of the church as "communion," we have become increasingly aware of the multiple charismata of the non-ordained, we have reached a deeper appreciation of the diversity of the local churches, and we have moved closer to other Christian churches and communities. Indeed, we have progressed from insight to insight into the mysteries. We have come to an expanded vision that postulates new norms of action.

The initiative of the *motu proprio* in reforming the Code can point the way toward future reforms, not in the manner of restrictions but for the sake of enrichment.

The Issue of Definitive Teaching. In the last two decades one significant problem for Catholic theologians has been the emergence of propositions definitively taught by the magisterium of the Holy See, propositions that are not infallible but are irreformable. The issue cannot be fully expounded here, but its complexity can be briefly shown.

The idea of definitive teaching, protected and defended now in both the Apostolic Letter and the *Commentary*, is called definitive in a new sense that has emerged gradually from the documents of the magisterium after Vatican Council II. Not that the expression was new: "teaching definitively" is used twice in *Lumen gentium* (25). There, the word "definitive," however, describes the nature of an infallible act either by the episcopal college or by the pope. If a pronouncement fulfills the rigorous criteria of infallibility, it is definitive; that is, it cannot change. It must be received with an act of faith.

The new use of the term by the magisterium of the Holy See is different: "definitive teaching" is not an infallible pronouncement, it does not require surrender in faith, yet it must be "embraced and held" as irreformable. There is the crux of the problem: how can a point of teaching not guaranteed by the assistance of the Spirit (as infallible definitions are) be irreformable?

This new category of definitive teaching (as such, not the specific content of any given proclamation) has not emerged from the crucible of an ecumenical council, nor is it the result of a thorough consultation among the bishops, nor has it been the fruit of critical debates among theologians. Yet it comes from an official source, *magisterium authenticum*. It is a significant new *datum* in the field of theology; it demands study and reflection.

An important note: definitive teaching in the new sense should not be confused with the so-called secondary objects of infallibility, which is a category developed at Vatican Council I and fully integrated into the understanding of the Tradition—with a capital *T*.

At present, the correct theological position seems to consist in acknowledging frankly that we are dealing with a case of developing doctrine. It concerns (first) the capacity of the church to speak definitively about a matter that is not obviously part of the revelation *and* (second) the obligation of the faithful to accept such a proclamation. As always, the passage of time is necessary (counted possibly in several pontificates), with the mentioned need for study and reflection to see and explain how, and how far, this new category is an articulation of our ancient tradition.

The *Commentary*. Signed by the Prefect and the Secretary of the Congregation for the Doctrine of Faith, the *Commentary* has been presented by many interpreters (including theologians of high repute) as "the document of the Congregation." This is a clear case of "upgrading" the authority of the communication—affecting (and falsifying) the binding force of its message. There is no reason to call this *Commentary* a "document of the Congregation." By the internal regulations of the offices of the Holy See, a declaration of this type ought to be ratified by the Congregation *as a collective body* (usually in a plenary session) *and* approved by the pope at least "in common form," which means that the pope agrees to its publication but does not make its content his own. The *Commentary* offers no evidence that such approvals have been granted; we must therefore conclude that we are dealing with a personal statement composed by the two highest ranking officials of the Congregation. We do not have an official proclamation by the Apostolic See.

It follows that assertions such as "the church has published a new list of infallibly taught doctrines" or that "the Holy See has reassessed the binding force of several points of doctrine" (and similar ones) published in the secular and religious press were incorrect. They represent an upgrading of the *Commentary*'s source and authority.

In truth, the church has not changed the binding force of any of its teaching. For instance, whatever the degree of authority of *Apostolicae curae* (the Letter of Leo XIII in which he declared the Anglican ordinations "utterly null and void") was before the publication of the *Commentary*, it is the same today. Admittedly, serious obstacles have arisen recently concerning the continuation of the dialogue between the Roman Catholic Church and the Anglican Church, yet there is no need to read the document *Ad tuendam fidem* as adding a new one—as it has been suggested by a few writers. The same reservation applies to every "example" (that is, point of doctrine) mentioned by Cardinal Ratzinger and Archbishop Bertone in their *Commentary*: the theological standing of every proposition on their list remains the same as it was before, no matter how they classified it.

The New Profession of Faith. In 1989 the Congregation for the Doctrine of Faith promulgated a new formula of "profession of faith" comprising the Nicene-Constantinopolitan Creed *and* three added paragraphs: one saying in substance that "I believe all that is divinely revealed even if not in the Creed," another stating that "I embrace and hold all that the church has definitively taught," and another again affirming that "I adhere with religious respect or submission, *obsequium*, to official proclamations even if they were not intended to be definitive." The ancient Creed and the additions have been brought into one integral structure that is now called the "profession of faith." All who accept ordination or an office in the church are bound to recite this complex Creed.

There is a difficulty. In this ecumenical age, the composition of a Christian profession of faith cannot be a purely internal affair of any church or communion: it has an ecumenical dimension. Vatican Council II made it clear that we are in partial communion with other Christian churches and ecclesial communions; they too belong to the church of Christ. The question then arises: does the imposition of the new profession of faith in the Roman Catholic Church serve the cause of unity?

In 451 "the sacred and universal synod" of Chalcedon decreed that "no one is permitted to produce, or even to write down or compose, any other Creed" than the one that we inherited from the Councils of Nicea and Constantinople. The Christian churches the world over have received the Chalcedonian decree with respect. They obeyed it for centuries; the only departure from it was the Latin addition of *filioque*. As it is well known, it was an addition strongly objected to by the Greeks, not only for its meaning but for being a violation of a sacred canon of an ecumenical council. If nothing else, ecclesiastical piety toward the Fathers of Chalcedon should restrain us from expanding their text. In truth, to add clauses to the ancient Creed referring to things that are not matters of faith, and then to call the whole structure a "profession of faith" is something altogether new. There is no precedent for it in all of Christian history.

A hard question is already arising among ecumenists of all churches and communities: is the intention of the Roman Catholic Church to make the acceptance of this new profession of faith a condition of unity?

Conclusion. The significance of the two documents can be summed up briefly:

- The Apostolic Letter does not introduce significant changes in our legal system; the *Commentary* is neither official magisterium nor does it contribute to the development of theology.
- Both documents stress the existence of definitive teaching in a new sense; neither of them gives an explanation of the nature of such teaching.
- Both documents support the new conception of a "profession of faith"; such a conception is undoubtedly against the decree of the Council of Chalcedon and is likely to be an obstacle to ecumenical progress.

• The Apostolic Letter in its introduction reveals a distrust in theologians: "To protect the Catholic faith against errors arising on the part of some of the Christian faithful, in particular among those who studiously dedicate themselves to the discipline of sacred theology. . ." Such a distrust (whatever its causes may be) is a wound within the body of the church; we all have a duty to seek the healing of this wound.

Finally, for the correct reception and interpretation of these (and many other) documents, we should recall that they are valuable and valid as far as they proclaim the revelation, bring the people of God closer to the divine mysteries, and create a favorable environment for the action of the Holy Spirit.

B.

Statement by Joseph Cardinal Ratzinger,
published in Stimmen der Zeit *217(1999) 169–72*
[Translated by Dr. Linda Maloney]

Statement [Stellungnahme]

Ladislas Orsy's article on the Motu Proprio *Ad tuendam fidem,*[1] which, happily, is written in a objective tone and without polemic, unfortunately contains some misinformation that requires correction.

1. Father Orsy assures us that new canons have become necessary because the category of definitively proposed teaching "as it appears now in official documents, did not exist [was not known]." He supports his assertion about the utter novelty of this category with the thesis that "definitive teaching" in the new sense must not be confused "with the so-called secondary object of infallibility"; the latter is said to be "a category developed at the first Vatican Council and fully integrated into the understanding of the Tradition." How the author arrived at this thesis is inexplicable. For naturally the second level of knowledge, the truths to be definitively maintained but not to be received with theological faith in the proper sense, means precisely

1. *Stimmen der Zeit*, November 1998, 735–40.

this category. The conclusions drawn from the unfounded division between the one and the other concept are therefore untenable.

A small imprecision scarcely worth mentioning in itself is that the author speaks of new canons, while the reality is that only a second paragraph has been added to Canon 750, with a reference to that paragraph added to Canon 1371. Since the issue is doctrinal and transcends ritual differences, the corresponding additions have been incorporated in the Code of the Eastern Churches as well.

2. I do not find it objective that Father Orsy constructs a contradiction between *Ad tuendam fidem* and Vatican II. According to him, the Council did not make use of threats and penalties because the Council Fathers "trusted that the faith would attract people through its own beauty and persuasive power," whereas the first reforms of the present Code of Canon Law do precisely that, namely, utter threats and impose penalties. Now, the Council Fathers, in making their decisions, naturally presupposed the validity of the order of church law as it was formulated by the then-applicable Code of Canon Law, which of course contained a section on penal law. At the same time, they also desired the reform of canon law called for by Pope John XXIII, in the knowledge that even a renewed code could not operate without penal laws. These might be eased and modernized but would still be a penal code. As a matter of fact, a large number of the world's bishops are now calling for a "sharpening" of the penal law, for example, in the case of priests who have been guilty of pedophilia, because the guarantee of the rights of the accused has become so powerful that the bishops feel themselves powerless in cases in which, for the sake of the faithful, they should have a clear authority to intervene. Besides, Father Orsy is surely aware that Paul practiced excommunication and thus applied ecclesiastical penal law, and that, for example, Matthew 18:15-17 shows that the Synoptic tradition likewise knew of penalties to enforce ecclesiastical discipline. It would be nice if people would in the future avoid such groundless contrasts, which create annoyance.

3. Let me note in passing that Father Orsy is not quite correct either in asserting that the possibility of reforming the Code of Canon Law is a novelty. Since the church is a living organism, this was foreseen from the beginning. Even in the case of the Code of 1917, a commission was established to provide for the authentic interpretation of the laws; it was intended that it would also insert into the Code such changes and additions as might become necessary. Similarly, the present Council for the Interpretation of Legislative Texts, while it is not itself empowered to make changes in the Code because it has no legislative authority, obviously has as one of its

functions to prepare for possible changes in the law and to be of counsel in the process of their preparation. It is clear that a further development of the law was envisioned from the outset.

4. The following assertion by the author is quite serious: "To add clauses to the ancient Creed referring to things that are not matters of faith, and then call the whole structure a 'profession of faith,' is something altogether new. There is no precedent for it in all of Christian history." Unfortunately, it seems that Father Orsy is somewhat cavalier in his assertions about what is a novelty. Had he searched his historical knowledge it surely would have occurred to him that ever since the Reformation, Protestant pastors have been ordained on the basis of the ancient church creeds and the Reformation confessions; and in parallel on the Catholic side, the ancient church creeds took their place alongside the profession of faith of the Council of Trent, which under Pius X was further augmented by the oath against modernism. The construction of an incompatibility between such expansive texts and the decree of Chalcedon that no one is authorized to present a different confession of faith recalls those fifth-century Fathers who asserted that Constantinople and Chalcedon were incompatible with the definitive character of Nicea.

To return to the present: In 1987, in the spirit of Vatican II, the Tridentine profession of faith and the oath against modernism were replaced by a brief and summary addition to the profession of faith that articulated the significance of the doctrine of the sacraments, of the sacrifice of the Mass, and of the primacy of the pope, and in general expressed assent to the church's doctrine in the manner demanded by [the authority of] a given doctrine. No one at that time criticized the replacement of the two long texts, which had become problematic from certain points of view, by a concise new formula of a few lines. On the contrary, it was regarded as a happy decision and a positive fruit of the Council. One could have objected to the formula of 1987 that it did not make a clear enough distinction among the degrees of assent and that it followed no clear criterion in its choice of the teachings that are not explicitly articulated in the Nicene-Constantinopolitan Creed. On the basis of such considerations a new version was composed that now distinguished clearly among theological faith in the proper sense, "ecclesiastical faith" corresponding to the "secondary objects of revelation," and "religious reverence" (*obsequium religiosum*) toward the non-infallible magisterium. This new, three-part extension to the profession of the ancient church was put in force on 9 January 1989, thus about ten years ago. Hence there has been at least a decade during which the distinctions among the levels [of teaching and assent] could have been discussed; why this did not happen in Germany, I cannot say. In any case, nothing was there asserted as a matter of faith that is not such; the very purpose of the formula was to distinguish the specific levels of assent.

5. I am happy that I can largely agree with Father Orsy's remarks on at least one point, namely, regarding the "explanatory commentary." While the whole text was composed by the Congregation, its successive stages of development were presented to the College of Cardinals, and its final version was approved by them. It also received the approval of the Holy Father. But all were agreed that the text in itself was given no binding force; rather, it was only offered as a help for understanding and was not to be published as an independent document of the Congregation. However, the particular form of its publication was purposely chosen to indicate that it was not a private work of the Prefect and the Secretary of the Congregation, but instead was an authorized aid to understanding the texts. That is subject to criticism, and here Father Orsy might well have been right in saying that such a genre is something altogether new. But why not? In any case, the conclusion Father Orsy has drawn from this, namely, that the examples [of doctrinal propositions] included in this text have no more weight than they had before, is correct. The intention was to list only examples whose degree of binding authority has been determined either by documents of the magisterium or by the consensus of the *auctores probati*. To that extent none need feel themselves restricted or subjected to authoritarian pressure by this text.

I regret that an essay that should have contributed to the objective character of the debate contains some rather grave errors, and I hope that these clarifications may lead to a better understanding of the document published in the summer of 1998, which has been rather too hastily criticized.

Joseph Cardinal Ratzinger

C.

Response by Ladislas Orsy,
published in Stimmen der Zeit *217 (1999) 305–16*
[English by the author]

Response to Cardinal Ratzinger
[Antwort an Kardinal Ratzinger]

I thank Cardinal Ratzinger for his communication and for giving me the opportunity to reflect at greater depth on the issues under discussion. He graciously recognizes that my original contribution was written "happily in an objective manner and without polemics." I intend to continue in the same manner.

Right from the beginning to the very end of this article, the reader should be aware that this exchange is not about the acceptance of the articles of faith but about faith seeking understanding, to use an expression of St. Anselm of Canterbury. The deposit of faith is fully accepted, the authentic magisterium is respected. The debate is about the interpretation of historical and theological data. It is a communication of insights and judgments on a level where human minds are struggling with the intelligence of divine mysteries.

The reader should also be aware that the concern about the nature of "definitive doctrine" is spread far and wide in the theological community. The importance of the issue has been forcefully stated by the French Jesuit theologian Bernard Sesboüé in reference to *Ad tuendam fidem*:

> No bishop, no priest, no cleric should remain unconcerned about a document that potentially carries such heavy consequences for ecclesiology; it is an effort to "put in place" [establish, construct] an ecclesiology.

The reason for this call to be concerned is the following:

> We are in the presence of a new domain of the exercise of the infallibility of the church.[1]

In other terms, the publication of *Ad tuendam fidem* is virtually as momentous as was the definition of papal infallibility at Vatican Council I.

If that is true, we are indeed witnessing a development that has heavy consequences for the internal life of the church, for the ecumenical movement, and for the correct presentation of the church to the human family.

---

1. See *Etudes*, October 1988, pp. 357, 359.

In responding to Cardinal Ratzinger, I shall follow his numbering of the topics.

1. The Category of "Definitive Teaching"

The central and principal issue in this debate, as it is perceived by many theologians (including Bernard Sesboüé), is the following: *Has there been an extension of the doctrine of the papal infallibility by the introduction of the category of "definitive teaching"?* If yes, we are indeed dealing with a development of doctrine as momentous as the first definition of infallibility by Vatican Council I; if not, we still have the task of determining the precise standing (authority, weight, theological note) of the *category* of "definitive teaching" which has been made part of the official teaching of the Holy See.

The resolution of this issue requires an examination of the pertinent historical and doctrinal data. A detailed and exhaustive study, however, within the framework of this article is not possible; yet a substantial demonstration is necessary otherwise the conclusion will not be convincing. I intend to give such a brief but substantial answer. It will be an attempt to disentangle the elements of a complicated problem and to offer a reasonable solution; a solution that is no more than a theological opinion and a contribution to a much larger debate. Also I feel that I can do better justice to the concerns of the cardinal—and to the topic itself—by a concise systematic exposition rather than by reflecting on a few particular points.

The debate is, of course, necessary. Many of our beliefs and convictions reached maturity and enabled the magisterium to reach a final decision because the issues were thoroughly discussed "in the schools." This is how the dogma of the immaculate conception, or papal infallibility, or more recently the doctrine of episcopal collegiality has become part of our Catholic beliefs. There is no reason why the category of definitive teaching should not go through this traditional and venerable process.

Throughout my presentation, I shall progress by raising questions. The first one, the point of departure, is historical: *What is the doctrine of Vatican Councils I and II on papal infallibility?*

There is an enormous amount of literature on this question; for our purposes it should be enough to answer it in a summary way.

Due to the assistance of the Spirit, the pope has the capacity to be an *infallible* witness of the revelation entrusted to the whole church; he can infallibly testify through *a solemn ex cathedra* definition; the proper object of his witnessing is the *revelation*; the faithful, to keep their communion with the church intact, have the obligation to receive his testimony with an *act of faith.* The peaceful and universal reception of a definition by the faithful is the authentic sign that the pope has spoken in the Spirit.

Since our inquiry centers on the question of whether or not the scope of the pope's infallibility has been extended, we should pay special attention to the object of infallibility as it was determined by the two Vatican Councils. For this, we have the statement of Gérard Philips who has thoroughly researched the mind of Vatican Council I and played a major role in the drafting of the Dogmatic Constitution on the Church, *Lumen gentium,* at Vatican Council II. He writes (my translation):

> Vatican Council I has occupied itself with [the *object* of infallibility] only tangentially. . . . The Constitution *Pastor aeternus,* Chapter 4, affirms simply that the assistance of the Holy Spirit is assured to the successor of Peter to conserve religiously and to proclaim faithfully [*sancte custodire et fideliter exponere*] the revealed doctrine. The Fathers of Vatican Council II specify today that the privilege of infallibility extends as far as the conservation and proclamation of the deposit of the faith entrusted to the church requires it. That far and no further. Once this limit is set, it includes a certain number of fundamental truths determined by philosophy as far as they are expressions of universal human experience. If someone, for example, held that human reason is forever unable to grasp truth with certainty, logically, he could not accept an article of faith either. Total relativism or agnosticism is not condemned by the revelation for the simple reason that neither the Scriptures nor the early church has come across a similar error. The theologians include under the same title of "indirect object" of infallibility a whole series of other elements, among them those which they call dogmatic facts. *All this belongs to the domain of professional theology; the Council itself is content to affirm the basic principle; the rest it leaves to the care of technical treatises.*[2]

That is, for Vatican Council I, the object of an infallible definition extended as far as the revelation, no more, no less. The Council did not wish to pronounce any further. Whatever teaching and knowledge existed beyond that field was left to professional theologians to explain and to qualify. On the basis of Gasser's well-known report, the Council Fathers understood but did not define that—if the need ever arose—the pope could exercise his infallibility with a solemn *ex cathedra* act to affirm a truth that is not explicitly in the revelation but is absolutely necessary to safeguard it.

Vatican Council II confirmed that the privilege of infallibility extended as far as the preservation and proclamation of the revelation demanded it.

---

2. Gérard Philips, *L'Eglise et son mystère*, vol. 1 (Paris: Desclée, 1967) 327–28; emphasis is mine.

Both councils were clear that a solemn *ex cathedra* act was the sign of an infallible definition.

Thus, the two Vatican Councils left us with two distinct levels of knowledge, one infallibly defined, another not defined. The second level was a complex continuum. The theologians had the task of handling it. They did, and they assigned differing authorities (theological notes) to various parts of it. They qualified some propositions as being of "catholic faith," and they called others "theological opinions." (To speak of "levels of knowledge" is, of course, figurative speech; some theologians prefer to use the term "parcels" for the same classification; the French introduced the word "baskets," *corbeilles de connaissance.*)

From the Councils we turn to the recent documents of the Holy See, especially to *Ad tuendam fidem*: they speak with authority of the theological reality of definitive teaching. *What is this category?* We can find the answer in the *Commentary* by Cardinal Ratzinger and Archbishop Bertone; I shall follow them closely, often word by word. They introduce their explanation by comparing the nature of definitive teaching with that of infallible definition.

What is the capacity of the magisterium? How far does the privilege of infallibility extend? The magisterium has the capacity to teach infallibly both doctrine divinely revealed and doctrine to be held definitively. In each case, the magisterium can teach either with an act that is defining or with an act that is not defining. If the act is "defining," the magisterium is teaching *ex cathedra* with a solemn definition; if the act is "not defining" (that is, a proposition is stated definitively), the magisterium is still teaching infallibly. It follows that the infallibility of the magisterium can become operational either with a solemn definition or with a definitive statement.

Comment: papal infallibility is operational in definitive statements; no solemn *ex cathedra* act is required.

What are the objects of definitive statements? They are points of doctrine that determine dogmas or norms of morality and are necessary for keeping and expounding the deposit of faith but are not proposed by the magisterium as formally revealed. Such teachings are linked to the revelation either by historical relationship or by logical connection.

What is the theological standing (weight, authority) of propositions definitively taught? They are irreformable. They can, therefore, be solemnly defined by the pope when he speaks *ex cathedra* or by the college of bishops gathered in council; they can be stated infallibly by the ordinary and universal magisterium; the same magisterium can propose them as dogmas.

What is the obligation of the faithful? The faithful should respond to the solemn definitions and to the "definitive declarations" with firm and definitive assent based on faith in the Holy Spirit who confers the charism of infallibility on the magisterium. There is no difference in the *nature* of the assent owed to revealed doctrine and to the doctrine to be held definitively: in each case the assent must be full and irrevocable.

The assent, however, in the case of revelation is based on faith in the authority of the Word of God; in the case of definitive teaching it is based on faith in the assistance of the Holy Spirit to the magisterium, the Spirit who endows the magisterium with the charism of infallibility.

What would be the consequence of the rejection of a point of doctrine definitively stated? It would be the loss of full communion with the Catholic Church—so states the *Commentary*.

Comment: Traditionally, the loss of full communion cannot mean anything else than schism or heresy.

Is there a difference between the doctrine of the Councils and that of the Commentary? Yes, the evidence is compelling and the conclusion is inevitable: a development has taken place. With the introduction of the category of definitive teaching, we have three levels (parcels, *corbeilles*) of knowledge: the first contains propositions defined, the second contains teachings definitively proclaimed, and the third contains other official pronouncements of the church.

The category of definitive teaching as it is presented in the *Commentary* is new.

The scope of papal infallibility, however, has been extended only if this new category has virtually the same characteristics as the first one. Hence the question: *Is there a real difference between infallible definitions and definitive statements?*

To answer this question, we must compare them. To compare them, we must know the nature (or the "essence" in scholastic language) of each type of teaching.

No need to delay with the doctrine of infallible teaching as it emerges from the two Vatican Councils, for many reliable explanations exist.[3] For the theory of definitive teaching we have ample information in the *Commentary*. A definitive statement has all the essential characteristics of an infallible definition. In each case the truth of a proposition is assured by the

---

3. See, e.g., Gérard Philips, *L'Eglise et son mystère*, 317 ff.

assistance of the Holy Spirit, the teaching is irreformable, and the acceptance of it is a condition of full communion.

Again, the evidence is compelling and the conclusion is inescapable: the *Commentary* presents the nature of definitive teaching (no matter which vocabulary is used) as equivalent to that of an infallible *ex cathedra* definition. Both are equally irreformable (there are no degrees in irreformability); both are irreformable because of the assistance of the Holy Spirit (there is no purely human way of reaching irreformability); both demand assent to keep the communion intact (there are no degrees in full communion). Bernard Sesboüé writes:

> The key word that conveys the intention of the text [of the document *Ad tuendam fidem*] is the word *definitive*. Now, the terms *definitive, irreformable, and infallible* are interchangeable [they have a common meaning]. We are therefore, in the presence of a new domain of the exercise in the infallibility of the church.[4]

This text is so important that for the sake of accuracy it should be quoted in the original.

> *Le mot clé qui résume l'intention du texte, est ici celui de définitif. Or les notions de définitif, d'irréformable et d'infallible communiquent entre elles. Nous sommes donc en présence de la revendication d'un nouveau domaine de l'exercice de l'infallibilité de l'Eglise.*

If there are differences between the two types of teaching, they are found in modalities. In the case of an infallible definition the pope must speak solemnly *ex cathedra* and leave no doubt about his intention. In the case of a definitive teaching it is enough for him to indicate that his statement is intended to be definitive; no more is required. In the case of an infallible definition, faith focuses on the word of God; in the case of a definitive statement faith focuses on the magisterium assisted by the Spirit. The end result is the same: an irreformable decision with the assistance of the Spirit is essential for full communion.

All considered, *it would follow* that the doctrine of "definitive teaching" (as explained in the *Commentary*) opens a new and vast field for infallible teaching. *If that is correct*, there is a practical need to adjust our textbooks of ecclesiology; there is also a need to revise our apologetics. We can no longer say that the pope is infallible in those rare and solemn instances when speaking *ex cathedra* he intends to define an article of faith. We must say in

---

4. *Etudes, loc. cit.,* p. 359.

all honesty that the field is broader. The pope is infallible whenever he intends to make a definitive statement.

To know all this conceptually is not enough. We need to realize what the implementation of this new doctrine would mean in practice. This can be shown by construing a hypothetical case on the basis of the *Commentary*. There is the issue of the validity of the Anglican orders. As it is now, not many theologians would be of the opinion that *Apostolicae curae* of Leo XIII was an infallible definition. The *Commentary*, however, lists it as an example of definitive teaching. It would follow that if a bishop, or a priest, or a theology professor ever deliberately and firmly stated that the decision of Leo XIII could be revised, he must be found guilty of breach of full communion with the church, and he must be deprived of his office and possibly excommunicated. Of course, any layperson persistently agreeing with him could be excommunicated as well.

I said cautiously *it would follow*, and I remarked conditionally *if that is correct* because there remains one substantial and thorny question: *What is the theological standing of the category of definitive teaching?* Not of any particular doctrine contained in it but of the new category itself.

This is the crux of this whole complicated problem. On the one hand, the official documents of the Holy See uphold—as described above—this new category with all its characteristics; on the other hand, as yet, no pope, no council has infallibly approved of it.

Now there is the traditional rule of interpretation of doctrine incorporated into canon law but certainly a norm more theological than legal: "No doctrine is understood as defined infallibly unless this is manifestly evident" (Canon 749 § 3).

This canon has a double effect on our considerations: it leads us to a conclusive statement and invites us to do further research.

The conclusive statement is that the second category of knowledge with all its characteristics as it is described in the *Commentary* does not and cannot have the standing of an infallible definition. We need not believe that the scope of papal infallibility has been extended. We are on sound theological ground if we continue to profess the doctrine of the two councils and abide in theory and in practice by their definitions.

At the same time, we are invited (we have the obligation) to inquire further into the nature and theological authority of the category of definitive teaching. It has been presented to the church universal by the Holy See; it must be received with due *obsequium*, "respect." Yet, as of now, we do not have a full comprehension of its place in our Tradition. It represents a new development that demands a considered response from the part of the episcopate and the community of theologians.

We must look also carefully into the ecumenical consequences of the doctrine of definitive teaching. Are we really explaining a tradition commonly held with the Orthodox churches? Or are we unilaterally creating a new impediment to the reunion of the sister churches who all intend to be faithful to the one common Tradition?

2. The "Signs of the Times"

The cardinal states: "I do not find it objective that Fr. Orsy constructs an opposition [*contradiction*] between *Ad tuendam fidem* and Vatican II. According to him the Council did not make use of threats and penalties because the Council Fathers 'trusted that the faith would attract people through its own beauty and persuasive power' whereas the first reforms of the present Code of Canon Law does precisely that. It invokes threats and punishments." Then the cardinal concludes that I am against penal law in the church, and to make his point he brings up the case of priests who are guilty of pedophilia.

My statement was different. I never raised the question whether or not the church should have penal law, still less have I even remotely suggested that priests guilty of pedophilia should not be disciplined. This is what I have written:

> At some later age, a church historian will probably point out how much the "signs of the times" have changed from the years of Vatican Council II to the end of this century. The Fathers of the Council wanted no threats or punishments in their documents; they trusted that faith will attract by its own beauty and persuasive power. As it happens now, the first reform of the present Code of Canon Law includes precisely that, threat and punishment.

I spoke of a change in the "signs of the times." To show that such change has occurred, here are two texts animated by different dynamics.

First, a quote from the address of *Pope John XXIII to the Council Fathers at the solemn opening of Vatican Council II, on October 11, 1962*:

> The church has always opposed errors. Frequently she has condemned them with the greatest severity. Nowadays, however, the spouse of Christ prefers to make use of the medicine of mercy rather than that of severity. She considers that she meets the needs of the present day by demonstrating the validity of her teaching rather than by condemnations. . . . That being so, the Catholic Church, raising the torch of religious truth by means of this ecumenical coun-

cil, desires to show herself to be the loving mother of all, benign, patient, full of mercy and goodness toward the children separated from her. . . . She opens the fountain of her life-giving doctrine which allows men, enlightened by the light of Christ, to understand well what they really are, what their lofty dignity and their purpose are, and, finally, through her children, she spreads everywhere the fullness of Christian charity, than which nothing is more effective in eradicating the seeds of discord, nothing more efficacious in promoting concord, just peace and the brotherly unity of all.[5]

Second, here is the opening paragraph of the Apostolic Letter *Ad tuendam fidem*:

To protect the Catholic faith against errors arising from the part of some of the Christian faithful, in particular from those who studiously dedicate themselves to the discipline of sacred theology, it appeared highly necessary to us, whose principal task is to confirm his brethren in faith (cf. Lk 22:32), to add [new] norms to the text of the presently valid *Code of Canon Law* and the *Code of Canons of the Eastern Churches*, in order to impose expressly the duty to preserve the truths proposed definitively by the magisterium of the church, and, concerning the same matter, to institute canonical sanctions [against the violators].

Concerning the need for penal law in the church: not once, in all my writings and lectures over forty years, have I stated that the church should have no penal law or that the penalty of excommunication should be altogether abolished. Interestingly, the cardinal refers approvingly to St. Paul; so do I in my book *Theology and Canon Law*, in a chapter critical of Sohm's theory: "Paul did not hesitate to give directions to the Corinthians, and he did so quite forcefully."[6]

In reference to excommunication, however, I have consistently held (and do hold) as follows: (1) Automatic excommunication *(latae sententiae)* should have no place in modern canon law because it is an anachronism; it compels a person to be the accused and the judge in his own case and it allows persons and communities to be condemned without the benefit of a hearing. Such a procedure is hardly in harmony with the Scriptures, and it offends contemporary sensitivities concerning human rights. (2) In our age, with *doctrinal matters* excommunication is not an effective policy to lead an errant soul back to the "obedience of faith." St. Peter Canisius, a

---

5. *Council Daybook* (Washington DC: National Catholic Welfare Conference, 1965) 27–28.

6. Ladislas Orsy, *Theology and Canon Law: New Horizons for Legislation and Interpretation* (Collegeville, MN: Liturgical Press, 1992) 183.

person vastly experienced in dealing with rebellion against faith, pleaded repeatedly with his superiors to do what they could to convince the Roman authorities not to use the weapon of excommunication against the Reformers; it only consummated a breach that perhaps could have been healed. His respected biographer, James Brodrick, writes:

> The Bull, *In Coena Domini*, [by Pius IV] which was so named because issued afresh each Holy Thursday, made him [Peter Canisius] very sad when it reached him in April, 1564, as it contained nothing but threats and prohibitions. "Would to God," he wrote, "that we could find some means of helping both pastors and people in the present great corruption, especially as every mortal thing seems full of excommunications. Nobody cares to give a little aid and consolation to the unhappy pastors who still sweat and labor for the religion that is dear to them."

This was, Brodrick continues, "an old complaint" of the Saint who desired "to secure a more kindly treatment for Germans in the matter of ecclesiastical censures, and to obtain greater consideration in Rome for parish priests who desire and are able to help the Catholic cause."[7]

3. The Reform of the Code of Canon Law

The cardinal states: "Fr. Orsy is not quite correct either in asserting that the possibility of reforming the Code of Canon Law is a novelty."

In truth, I have not discussed the *possibility* of the reform of the Codex at all. All theologians and canon lawyers know that such possibility exists. I was simply reporting a fact: the first step in a reform process had been taken.

Legal historians know well that every legislator is reluctant to undertake the first step that breaks the original unity of a code; it can convey a message of instability. There is the ancient adage: *mutatio legis odiosa*, "change of law is odious." For this reason the first change has a symbolic value. It signals that the legislator is willing and ready to undertake necessary reforms. In this sense I wrote, "the initiative itself of inserting new norms into the Code has a positive dimension"—even if it is a threat of punishment.

Vatican Council II has identified immense sources of vital energies in the church, such as the graces and charismata of baptized laypersons, the collegial power of the episcopate, the unique value of the local churches or of the churches in a common cultural region, and the particular gifts of the

---

7. James Brodrick, *Saint Peter Canisius* (London: Sheed and Ward, 1938) 611–12.

Spirit to non-Catholic Christian churches and communities. Such energies cry out for appropriate legal structure. To channel and to insert them into the Code should be easier now. And a cause for joy that the process of adjusting our laws to new theological insights has begun.

4. The Profession of Faith

Cardinal Ratzinger does not share my concern about keeping the ancient and sacred name of "profession of faith," *symbolum fidei*, precisely and exclusively for that: articles of faith.

I have raised the issue of the new profession of faith in an ecumenical context, especially in relation to our obligation to promote the union of Christian churches. I asked whether or not the imposition of the new profession of faith in the Roman Catholic Church serves the cause of unity. I reported the concern of the ecumenists of other Christian churches: they are wondering if the Roman Catholic Church intends to make the new profession a condition of reunion.

The fundamental problem with the new profession is that it includes articles of faith and matters that are not of faith; it does not have an organically unified content. For this reason it is not traditional. Yet, the whole complex is officially called profession of faith. The traditional purpose of a *symbolum fidei* has always been *to set apart the articles of faith from all other knowledge*, never to contain and distinguish different levels of knowledge.

The Protestant professions the cardinal invoked to show that there is a precedent for such an unusual structure in a profession of faith are not suitable examples. Protestant professions were not formulated in communion with the universal episcopate (including the See of Peter), and they were never intended to bind the faithful in the same way as the ancient *symbola*. They were considered by the Reformers themselves not as *norma normans*, rule that binds, but as *norma normata*, rule that is under another rule, in this case under the rules of private judgment and of the *sola scriptura*.

Of course new professions of faith were formulated in the West, but as far as I am able to ascertain they all were intended to focus on articles of faith—as they were known at that stage of doctrinal development. Besides, all of them had a somewhat limited life. Here and now, however, we are speaking of an addition to the Nicene-Constantinopolitan Creed, the Creed that has been, and is, a permanent living bond among separated Christian churches and ecclesial communities.

Can we ever forget the bitter resentment that the insertion of *filioque* into the Creed has generated throughout the Orthodox churches, a resentment that lingered for more than a millennium and which by the grace of God is being healed in our days? Is this the time to add new paragraphs to a sacred text and call the whole new formula *symbolum fidei*? If one day God in his mercy brings us to the threshold of union, shall we insist that the patriarchs, metropolitans, and bishops of the Orthodox churches must recite our new profession of faith? How does all this correspond to the spirit of the encyclical *Ut unum sint?*

The ecumenical concern remains.

5. The *Commentary*

Theologians and canon lawyers the world over will be grateful to the cardinal for the clarification of the theological authority of the *Commentary*. Although the Congregation and the pope had it *gebilligt*, that is, "reviewed" it, but not in a formal sense, they decided not to publish it as an official document of the Holy See.

Be that as it may, it is a document of importance. I do not know of any other where the whole theology of the category of the definitive teaching is explained so thoroughly.

No theologian should take this explanation lightly, but no theologian should grant it final authority. An analogy comes into my mind: the weight of this *Commentary* may be similar to that of the draft documents of Vatican Council II which had been approved by the central preparatory commission and the pope himself and declared worthy to be submitted to the judgment of the Council. As we know the Council radically changed them.

We may be in a similar situation. We have a document that originated in the offices of the Holy See, a document that contains matters of grave concern for the universal church. It needs now the scrutiny of the universal episcopate, the scholarly dialectics of the theological community, and the probing of its depth by the *sensus fidelium*.

At the center of such a scrutiny (*Prüfung*) must be, undoubtedly, the nature of the category of definitive teaching. It is affirmed in the official documents of the Holy See; hence it must be respected. It is hardly understood in the community of theologians; hence it must be explained. Cardinal Ratzinger sees this category as the "receptacle" of truth guaranteed by the Holy Spirit's assistance to the magisterium; the theologian Peter Hünermann finds the same approach an "aggravating simplification" (*eine gravierende Simplifizierung*), and he draws the attention to the "creaturely content" (*kreaturliche Sachverhalte*) of the propositions presented as being in this category.[8]

8. Cf. Herder Korrespondenz 1998, 458, 459.

There is nothing astounding that such an important development causes a great deal of controversy: we are struggling with the understanding of the operations of the church of God that is a great mystery—the words of St. Paul. The Spirit of God is not with us less in creative dialogues than in final decisions; the search for truth is not less holy than truth itself.

Conclusion

I want to thank Cardinal Ratzinger again for the opportunity of this exchange. Differences undoubtedly will remain but they are well within the parameters of faith. Cardinal Newman's *Essay on the Development of Christian Doctrine* may help us to understand, handle, and even respect such differences. He insists throughout his *Essay* that the "Christian idea" is so rich and has so many facets that no human person, no matter how holy or learned, can receive, perceive, and express all its aspects; in Newman's mind not even one of the apostles could have done it. We all share in these riches. "Christianity is dogmatical, devotional, practical, all at once; it is esoteric and exoteric; it is indulgent and strict; it is light and dark; it is love, and it is fear." As our understanding struggles with such an immense gift, "new lights will be brought to bear upon the original statements of the doctrine put forward; judgments and aspects will accumulate" until there emerges "the complete image as seen in combination of diversified aspects, with the suggestions and corrections of many minds, and the illustration of many experiences" (chapter 1, section 1).

This is the only way that faith can seek and find understanding.

D.

Response by Joseph Cardinal Ratzinger,
published in Stimmen der Zeit 217 (1999) 420–422
[Translated by Dr. Linda Maloney]

Closing Statement to the Debate with Father Orsy *
[Schlusswort zur Debatte mit Pater Orsy]

I welcome Fr. Orsy's response to my critique of his essay published in
the November 1998 issue of *Stimmen der Zeit*; it clarifies his intentions and
thus makes the content of his article easier to understand. His explanations
are helpful in many respects, but on a number of points I must still express
my disagreement.

[1. The Category of "Definitive Teaching"]

Fr. Orsy's extensive reflections concerning the category of "definitive teaching" are for me largely incomprehensible. He affirms again, as he did in his
first article, that with this category a new and previously unknown level of
knowledge has been created. In this, I cannot follow him at all. He offers not
a single word in response to my stated opinion that this category is equivalent
to the long-recognized doctrine of the "secondary objects of infallibility."

Archbishop Pilarczyk [of Cincinnati], in an important lecture he gave at
the joint meeting of the Congregation for the Doctrine of Faith and of the
Doctrinal Commission [of the Bishops' Conferences] of North America
and Oceania, thoroughly reviewed the issue once again; I wish to refer in
advance to that lecture, which will be published soon together with the
other lectures from that symposium. In his talk the archbishop recalled the
distinction, formulated at the First Vatican Council, between *credenda* and
tenenda; it is precisely this "duality" that is represented by the distinction
between the first and second levels of knowing that has been incorporated
into the new, extended form of the profession of faith.

As regards the form of the model text referred to, the Archbishop of
Cincinnati pointed out that Pius IX, in opposing Döllinger's thesis that only
truths formally defined can be regarded as dogmatic teaching of the church,
immediately proposed the idea that the ordinary and universal teaching of
the bishops can also be the basis for required belief (DS 2879 [*Letter to the*

---

* The subtitles in brackets are explanatory insertions by the translator. Also, some long
paragraphs in the original are broken up into shorter ones in the translation.

Archbishop of Münich-Freising: Tuas libenter]; reaffirmed at Vatican Council I, DS 3011 [*Dogmatic Constitution on Faith: Dei Filius*]). Finally, following Sullivan, Archbishop Pilarczyk quoted the deliberations of the theological commission of Vatican Council II, affirming the duality of *credenda* and *tenenda* as well as that this is the basis for the distinction between the two levels in the profession of faith.

[2. Punishment]

I cannot understand how Fr. Orsy can say that on the ground of the denial of a definitive teaching someone could be "guilty of a breach of full communion with the church, and he must be deprived of his office and possibly excommunicated." The *motu proprio* has, in this regard, taken as its special purpose to create greater clarity about the legal consequences of a denial of definitive teaching by means of an addition to the Code of Canon Law. It prescribed the same sanction for this as for a violation of the duty of *obsequium religiosum*, that is, for the third level of assent: *iusta poena puniatur* [to be punished by just penalty]. That in a particular case, because of its special character, the loss of office might be the "just punishment" is another matter entirely. But to present this in a horror scenario as if it were a regular event is incompatible with the clear text of the *motu proprio*.

[3. Signs of the Times]

Fr. Orsy's observations concerning the signs of the times also remain incomprehensible for me. In his first article he wrote that the Fathers of Vatican II were against threats and punishments, but that the first "reform" of the existing Code of Canon Law does precisely that. I explained (against his view) that there were two distinct levels at issue; on the one hand the orientation of the conciliar documents taken as a whole, on the other hand the existence of penal law in the church. In no way did I insinuate that Fr. Orsy is altogether against penal law. I only called attention to the difference between the two levels and showed that the existence and further development of penal law in the church cannot be presented as being contrary to the intentions of Vatican Council II. Fr. Orsy asserted this contradiction; I denied it—nothing more, nothing less. Although his observations concerning the signs of the times are in themselves interesting, they change nothing in this regard.

[4. The New Profession of Faith]

Finally, I cannot see as in any way relevant what Fr. Orsy thinks he needs to say in defense of his position regarding the "new profession of faith." I shall not enter into all the details, but only offer some remarks. First, the parallel with the *filioque* is absolutely incorrect. What disturbed the Greeks (apart from the issue of content) was the insertion of an additional word into the Nicene-Constantinopolitan Creed itself. This cannot be the issue here.

Further, Fr. Orsy tells us that until now the various professions of faith formulated in the West have in a sense had a limited life span, but now it is different. How, then? Who has ever asserted that this threefold expanded formula must be retained from now on and for eternity? As the earlier formulas of the post-Tridentine period, including the one from 1967, could be replaced by a text that better corresponded to new requirements, it is of course possible for the same to happen to the present formula when, in the same or similar way, new conditions arise.

As regards the Protestant professions of faith, it is obvious that the comparison I offered has its limits. But within those limits it is correct. Moreover, the threefold formula has no content and to that extent is necessarily a *norma normata* [roughly: a general framework] in that it refers to the content of normative doctrinal pronouncements. It is clear, therefore, that this formula is not of the same type as the Nicene-Constantinopolitan Creed. Rather, it adds to the Creed a provision for the development of doctrine and for the different degrees of obligation.

Finally, a remark concerning the Ecumene: in ecumenical dialogue, beyond Nicea, subsequent doctrinal developments and the question of their binding force are always subject to discussion, quite independently of the threefold formula. The formula itself is not creating any new problem; at most it is a reminder of the problems of doctrinal development and the teaching office, which are well known to every ecumenist.

[5. Agreement]

All the more I am able to agree, in conclusion, with the outlook Fr. Orsy, with reference to Cardinal Newman, describes at the end of his article. Indeed, Cardinal Newman is the great teacher in matters concerning the development of faith. We can always learn something new from him.

CONCLUDING NOTE BY LADISLAS ORSY

After Cardinal Ratzinger's last statement, in consultation with the editor of *Stimmen der Zeit*, I arrived at the judgment that no immediate response was warranted; rather, a pause for reflection was needed. The debate achieved its primary purpose. It established that the nature of "definitive doctrine" as it is proposed in the *Motu Proprio* and explained in its official *Commentary* can be the object of a legitimate public debate. At the center of an exchange is the question of whether the contents of definitive doctrine, as the examples in the *Commentary* illustrate them, are or are not identical with the (so-named) "secondary objects of infallibility" envisaged by Vatican Council I (cf., e.g., DS 3069) that the faithful must accept and hold.

The debate ought to be resumed, both a difficult and a delicate task.

The question, however, is not only a matter for disputation, because the Holy See enacted laws and ordinances to enforce the acceptance of definitive doctrines as defined in *Ad tuendam fidem* and as exemplified in the *Commentary*. Such practical provisions are already effectively at work and, in a subtle but forceful way, are shaping the church of the future. The new and expanded Profession of Faith and the recent Oath of Fidelity[10] is required now, not only from candidates for the sacrament of orders, but also from nominees to ecclesiastical offices—even minor ones. Persons reluctant to pronounce the new Profession of Faith or take the Oath of Fidelity are not punished, but they are excluded from important positions in the church; that is, their participation in the building of the church is restricted.[11] One can only wonder: Are two classes of Christians being created in the Roman Catholic Church, one with access to decision-making processes, another excluded from the same? Are the new requirements overshadowing the baptismal commitment? Is the distance between the clergy and the rest of the people increasing? Is the ancient adage "In necessaries unity, in doubts liberty, in all charity" (*In necessariis unitas, in dubiis libertas, in ominibus caritas*) still held in honor—not only abstractly but in the concrete order?

Questions abound, but they should do no harm. Faith is a compelling force, it seeks an understanding of the mysteries, *fides quaerit intellectum*; faith cannot

---

10. See AAS 81 (1989) 104–6.

11. I am reluctant to speak of "dissenters" because dissent is a vague term. It can imply a verifiable break with authentic *communio*. It can also be used for a legitimate theological position well within the *communio* of faith but different from an official one. Our theological discourse, official or personal, would highly benefit from abandoning the word "dissent" altogether and forever, and speaking simply and clearly of a breach of *communio* when faith is abandoned. Otherwise, we should follow and fully honor the adage, *"In necessariis unitas, in dubiis libertas, in omnibus caritas."*

be in any other way. But in the community of believers all such inquiries are rooted in, and sustained by, hope. No matter how much we struggle with obscurities, we are moving toward the light. We need our questions, as fragile and imperfect as they may be. Without them how could the Spirit of God shepherd us toward the full truth (cf. John 16:13)?

In the Service of the Holy Spirit
The Ecclesial Vocation of Canon Lawyers

For everything there is a season,
and a time for every matter under heaven. (Eccl 3:1)

T he words of the Preacher in Ecclesiastes apply also to canon lawyers. There is a time to conceive and to promulgate laws; there is a time to interpret and to implement them. But there should also be a season for exploring the ultimate meaning of the work of canon lawyers, that is, the meaning that brings sense into all that they do.

My aim is not to produce an abstract theological treatise and offer new theories. Rather, I wish to discover and clarify in a practical fashion the respective positions that the Spirit and lawyers have in the life of the church and the connections between these two operations.

The title of this piece, however, is not complete and an explanation is therefore in order. The expression "in the *service* of the Holy Spirit" is true but is not the full truth. It is true because human beings are the Spirit's servants, not masters of their own right. It is not the full truth because Christ raised his disciples to a lasting partnership with himself and with his Spirit: "No longer do I call you servants . . . I have called you friends . . ." (John 15:15). And because they are friends, they are also witnesses of Christ in partnership with the Spirit: "I shall send to you from the Father, even the Spirit of truth, who proceeds from the Father, he will bear witness to me; and you also are witnesses, because you have been with me from the beginning" (John 15:26-27).

The Spirit of God is the one who brings the church into existence and sustains it. The church, however, by divine design needs visible structures to be a community of human beings and to operate in a human way. This need is the foundation of the ecclesial vocation of canon lawyers: they are called to be *partners of the Spirit in building structures for the unfolding kingdom of God in human history.*

A more fitting title for these reflections could be *In "Partnership" with the Holy Spirit: The Ecclesial Vocation of Canon Lawyers*. My purpose throughout is to explore the significance of this relationship between the Holy Spirit and canon lawyers.

It may be an unusual inquiry—not frequent in canonical commentaries. Authors prefer to raise questions about "the nature of canon law" or "the obligations of canon lawyers," and then they proceed to formulate theories that define the "essence of the law" or the "substance" of the obligations of canon lawyers. While such discourses may be enlightening, they are not enough. Here and now, I wish to go beyond mere concepts and theories and focus my attention on persons, their operations, and their relationships.

The *dramatis personae* are, then, the Holy Spirit and canon lawyers.

There is a long-standing tradition in Christian theology that holds that the Holy Spirit is the personification of the inner *love* of God—as the Son is the personification of the inner *Word* of God. Thus, if the Spirit creates and re-creates the church throughout its history and holds its foundational structures together, those structures are the work of love.[1] Dante Alighieri wrote of "the Love that moves the sun and the other stars" (*Paradiso 33:145*). Inspired by him, we could speak of *Love that gives a human face to the church*.[2]

I use the term *canon lawyers* in an encompassing sense: it includes legislators, administrators, judges, and, of course, academic lawyers, all of whom effectively contribute to the legal life of the church.[3] I see them as the members of an organic social body, even if they are not organized into a guild or corporation. Their activities touch on every aspect of the life of laws, from their creation to their reception.

All that follows intends to display an integrated vision of the church. It affirms the creative work of the Spirit, and it asserts the role of human contribu-

---

1. If laws are for the well-being of the community, as they should be, then all laws, secular and religious, are more than justice. They are manifestations of the love that the scholastics called *amor benevolentiae*, "love that wants to give" or "love that wants to enrich the other." Virtues do not exclude each other; they blend and integrate into increasingly higher units. Thus justice becomes love. Justice could be defined as the minimum of charity.

2. Some foundational structures in the church are of divine institution and therefore permanent. Many others are built on "divine foundation" but of human construct; therefore they are marked by human intelligence and prudence. So they are changeable and often in need of reform.

3. "Canon lawyers" are here defined by their learning and expertise. In no way do I suggest that learning and expertise gives any "power to rule," *potestas regiminis*, which is sacramental and is required for authentic power to govern. I suggest, however, that even if someone has that power, he will not be able to "build the church" competently unless he has also the learning and expertise of a *iurisprudens*. Ordination gives power but not science—or prudence.

tion in building structures and providing norms for the community. In sum, the ecclesial vocation of canon lawyers consists in giving concrete expressions to the subtle aspirations of the Spirit—a call of the highest order.

A Pause for Clarification

At this point, a question emerges: If the ecclesial vocation of canon lawyers is to create, interpret, and implement laws, what is the role of hierarchy? Surely, in their ordination bishops are invested with power (*dynamis, exousia, potestas*) by the Holy Spirit. They and they alone have the right to create, to promulgate, to interpret, and to apply laws. Are they two contending groups? Not really: the two groups are complementary.

We hold that bishops, and they alone, have the authority to rule the church; no canon lawyer has such power. To rule the community *well*, however, requires learning and expertise that the sacrament of orders does not give. The organic nature of the social body of Christ reveals itself once more: there is interdependence among the members. Binding and loosing the people, *ligare et solvere*, are within the power of the bishops. Conceiving new laws, directing articulation of their texts, and forming judgments concerning the interplay of values when laws are implemented are certainly within the task of the experts.

The ecclesiastical vocation of canon lawyers ought to be understood in this framework. Through their learning they are partners to both the Holy Spirit and the hierarchy—although in different ways.[4]

The rest of my exposition falls into two parts organically linked. The first, "The Spirit in the Church," is a brief presentation of the timeless presence and operation of the Spirit in the church. The second, "Canon Lawyers in Partnership," speaks of the task of the canon lawyers in our times.

---

4. No one has ever stated more clearly and succinctly the difference between bishops and "doctors" than Aquinas. He discussed it within the framework of the two cathedras: To be promoted to an episcopal cathedra, the qualification required is to be eminent in charity. Ordination then confers eminence in power in relation to the faithful; power that the person did not possess before. To be promoted to a doctoral cathedra, sufficient learning, *scientia*, is necessary. The position offers an opportunity to use the knowledge and skill that a person possessed before (cf. *Quodl. 3, 9, c*).

Comments: Ordination gives no knowledge; no person becomes more learned by it. Competent government, however, especially in our contemporary church, demands a high degree of learning. It follows that ordinarily, unless the bishop has personally sufficient knowledge and skill, he needs the help of the "doctors" to govern well. (Of course, every bishop has the moral duty to govern well.)

In the church of Christ no member can stand and function alone; there is an interdependence among the organs as there is in one human body. Should this needed interchange be neglected, the whole body is bound to suffer.

THE SPIRIT IN THE CHURCH

I single out five prominent activities of the Spirit in the church. In all of them, the Spirit is the principal player. He gathers the faithful into an organic body and engenders life. In all of them, the same Spirit needs human agents to bring to a completion the divine initiatives.[5]

The Spirit is continuously creating the church.

We tend to assign a beginning to the existence of the church: the day of that Pentecost when the Holy Spirit was poured out on the disciples—the birth of the church. Then we easily assume that the community continued on its own accord thereafter. That is not the case. Today, as ever, we live in Pentecostal times: the Holy Spirit is being poured out on disciples no less than on that great day in Jerusalem. Here and now, the Spirit is creating the church and fills it with energy to grow in grace and wisdom.

The Spirit keeps the Word of God alive in the community and leads the people from insight to insight into its content.

The Spirit wants the community not only to preserve the Word but also to progress in the perception of the Word's internal riches. "When the Spirit of truth comes, he will guide you into all the truth . . . he will speak, and he will declare to you the things that are to come" (John 16:13).

The Spirit infuses energy into the people.

Energy, *energeia*, in early Christian literature was enabling power from above that leads to action and operation: a capacity that has its source in the divine.[6] In the concrete order, this is the pouring out of grace through the sacraments— and beyond the sacraments.

The Spirit intends to heal a divided church.

Today the great church of Christ is an internally wounded body. While the Spirit holds together all those who were baptized "in the name of Christ," their

---

5. A "hierarchical communion" is a structured communion; it demands legislation for its exercise. The primacy of Peter is of divine foundation, but for its effective practice laws of human creation are needed. The seven sacraments are God's saving deeds, but for their administration human norms are necessary.

6. For references see the entries *energeia, energeo, energema,* and *energes* in *A Greek-English Lexicon of the New Testament and Early Christian Literature,* ed. William Arndt and Wilbur Gingrich (Chicago: University of Chicago, 1952) 264–65.

different understanding of the Word pulls them apart and keeps them divided. They are one and they are not. They say "Jesus is the Lord," but they do not come together to give thanks and share his body and blood in one undivided sacrifice. In the last decades, however, an immense desire for unity has taken possession of many Christians the world over, a desire that could have only come from the Spirit.

The Spirit intends for the church to be a visible sign of God's saving will.

"God our Savior . . . desires all men to be saved and to come to the knowledge of truth" (1 Tim 2:3-4). Hence the church is a saving mystery and a human reality. As a human reality it has an image that the world can see and read. To fulfill its mission, the church must make sure that the image reflects the saving mystery: the humble simplicity of the Son of Man and the otherworldly glory of the risen Christ.

In all these activities the Spirit is the principal agent. He is like the master painter who provides firm outlines and then mandates the disciples to complete the picture.

CANON LAWYERS IN PARTNERSHIP

The New Testament speaks of "time," *kairos*, in several holy senses. Among them are welcome time, difficult time, and fruitful time.[7]

The coming years—decades, even centuries—should be a welcome time for those to whom the care of the church's legal life has been entrusted because it will bring them challenges that their predecessors have not known. The insights of Vatican Council II concerning the laity, episcopal collegiality, unity of Christian churches, and so forth will increasingly take possession of the minds and hearts of the faithful, and the need for appropriate structures will emerge with ever-greater urgency. A time that brings so much demand and opportunity should be a "welcome time" for those who are called to be partners with the Spirit.

Let us have no illusion: it will be a difficult time as well. We know in retrospect that the reception of every major council has been slow and painful. So is the reception of Vatican Council II, all the more so because its insights have consequences in the practical order and postulate a conversion in the habits of human thoughts and operations. This is the price the community must pay

---

7. Cf. the entry *kairos*, ibid., 395–96.

in exchange for deeper understanding of the mysteries and a more intense participation in them—and a blessed price it is.

Yet there should be no doubt: it shall be a fruitful time. As the energies latent in our dedicated laity, in the episcopal college, and in the church of Christ (now suffering from disunity) are given scope, there will be an abundant harvest of good fruit for the benefit of all. Our hope is well founded: the Spirit has taken the initiative.

Canon lawyers of our age are called to be laborers that usher in the Lord's times—"prepare the ways of the Lord!" But how should they prepare themselves for the task? What should their qualifications be? I present an image, *ikon*, which sums up the ecclesial vocation of a canon lawyer. It is an ideal; hence no one should be blamed for not having reached it. Yet no one should feel dispensed from striving for it. In doing so, there is a list of qualities that the ideal demands.

Awareness of the importance of the work to be done.

This awareness means a secure confidence in the value of the contribution that canon lawyers can make. Without such conviction they could hardly give themselves fully to the task.

Because Christ has granted the charism of unerring fidelity (infallibility) in matters of doctrine to his church, but has never promised that those who give practical directions to the community will act unfailingly with the highest degree of prudence in the matter of practical decisions, the official leaders of the church need persons eminent in the virtue of prudence, perceptive in gathering information, able to see behind appearances, and qualified to form critically grounded value judgments.

In the church to come, canon lawyers cannot be mere passive commentators of the law: both God in heaven and people on earth are expecting more from them.[8]

Respect for the freedom of the Spirit.

Law can invade the life of the church to such an extent that it impedes the communication of the Spirit. It is well known that, under the regime of the Code of 1917, the law for administering the sacrament of penance was so restrictive that the ministry of forgiveness has suffered. Also, the control over theologians

---

8. Schools of canon law have a duty to convey to students *the breadth and length and height and depth* (see Eph 3:18) of their vocation. The church cannot afford to train canon lawyers in the post-Tridentine mood anymore: the task waiting for them is much broader than that.

grew so tight that it impeded creative thinking. At Vatican Council II, many diocesan bishops complained that an excessive centralization in the universal church left little room (if any) for the development of local churches.

Sound "supernatural instinct" is required to recognize the freedom of the Spirit and to limit the domain of the law accordingly.[9]

Intelligence of faith.

In the church the external operations flow from, or are prompted by, the inner dynamism of divine mysteries. Since canon lawyers are called to give shape and form to such operations, they must be well acquainted with the theological nature of the mysteries. No one can follow the *ecclesial vocation* of a canon lawyer, nor give an *ecclesial interpretation* of the laws, unless he or she has had a personal encounter with the mysteries.[10] To conceive good laws for the administration and reception of the sacraments in a saving community, such intimate knowledge and experience is necessary.

Knowledge and expertise in the field of law.

Much of canon law consists of human norms for the reception of divine gifts. Thus, canon lawyers should be open to legal wisdom even when it comes from secular sources.[11] There is much in classical Roman law that can bring us fresh inspiration even today: its restraint in statutory legislation, its concise style, and its reliance on equitable rules can all be models for our canon law. There is wisdom in the common law of English origin too. It could teach us

9. In this matter we could learn a good deal from our sister churches in the East: throughout their history they have placed their trust more in the Spirit than in the law. It is important that the application of *Code of Canons for the Eastern Churches* should leave this precious tradition shared by all Eastern Christians intact. The hermeneutics for the understanding and implementation of that Code should be as different from the Latin Code as the spirit of Constantinople was different from that of Rome.

10. For background reading see Enrico Mazza, *Mystagogy: A Theology of Liturgy in the Patristic Age,* trans. from Italian (New York: Pueblo, 1989). The encounter with the divine mysteries in liturgy is the indispensable condition for the creation of ecclesial structures and norms for the administration and reception of the sacraments.

11. The legal system in the church has a dual origin; it is like a river with two sources. Since the church is a human community, structures and norms essential for the formation of a human community are relevant for the church. Since the church is the assembly of those who were "born of God," it is ruled also by laws of divine origin. Canon law has two natures blended into one organic body. "Monophysite" theories of canon law can never be satisfactory; either they will upgrade canon law unduly and claim that it is an entirely supernatural product, or they will downgrade it and assert that it is a secular reality.

effective ways to protect the rights of the faithful, it could help us to have work-ing norms for "due process," and it could suggest legal means to prevent undue delays in administration.

Canon lawyers versed in legal history and international jurisprudence can help the church to become more international (as it should be) even in its legal system.

A sense of the strengths and weakness of the community for which the law is intended.

Laws always operate in the concrete world: they are addressed to a given com-munity that has its own strengths and weaknesses. The ancient Hebrews under-stood this well. For them the "Law," *Torah*, had an educative task. Canon law, too, can have an educative task, but it should always take into account the dispositions of the people. Excessive demands often result in noncompliance.[12]

This sense for the concrete capacity of the people (a down-to-earth reality) is required in a competent canon lawyer just as much as their familiarity with the mysteries.

Ability to arbitrate when law and life meet.

When a law is imposed, an abstract, general, and impersonal norm is applied to a concrete, particular, and often personal situation. It is an encounter be-tween two universes: one concerned with an ideal uniformity, the other one with a practical necessity. From time to time, conflicts are bound to arise. No human law can be just in all cases, as Aristotle noted.[13] The clue to the resolu-tion of conflicts is in the correct assessment of the hierarchy of values and in setting the priorities accordingly. If the law loses in such a confrontation, it will not be a case of contempt of law but an act of respect for life.

Creative foresight.

Since the Spirit is creative, canon lawyers must be creative. They must criti-cally evaluate the existing laws and propose improvements. To plan for future legislation is their sacred obligation. The church is a dynamic community that is always in need of development. Past laws must be adjusted to present needs; present laws must be open to future demands. As we have it now, in the con-

---

12. Obviously, all this refers to human laws in the church.

13. See "Equity, a Corrective of Legal Justice," in Aristotle, *The Nicomachean Ethics*, trans. David Ross, 1137a32–1138a39 (Oxford: Oxford University Press, 1980) 132–34.

stitutional structures of the church no provision exists to assure an ongoing renewal of its laws. This serious omission, however, can be balanced by canon lawyers trained to use their imagination.

CONCLUSION

In these post–Vatican II years, the Catholic Church is a community enriched by new insights about the nature of the church and its mission in the world; it is also a community that is still waiting for structures and norms that will give full scope to those insights. Visionary insights generate expectations. Effective fulfillment of such expectations can come only from those who are invested with apostolic authority: Peter's successor and the other bishops to whom the Spirit has granted power to bind and to loose.

This power, however, by its very nature demands the learning and expertise that canon lawyers have. Under the impact of Vatican Council II, a new movement has emerged in the community of canon lawyers, a movement that is best described as a process of intellectual conversion, *metanoia*. This movement is bringing new questions and produces fresh responses in fulfilling the Spirit's intentions. "Faith seeks action," *fides quaerit actionem*.

Our time is our gift. A welcome time: yes. A difficult time: certainly. A fruitful time: that is our hope—in partnership with the Spirit.

Epilogue

For the church universal to receive the Council is to enter into the dynamics of the Council.

For communities and individuals to enter into the dynamics of the Council is to expose themselves to the ever-surprising action of the Spirit.

Whenever the Fathers gathered at St. Peter's Basilica, their prayer was the traditional exclamation, *Adsumus*—"we are present and listening."

Over four years the Spirit heard their cry and responded. Before our own eyes the promise of Jesus was fulfilled: "When the Spirit of truth comes, he will guide you into all the truth" (John 16:12).

Now it is the turn of the universal people to say, *Adsumus*, to be present and attentive, and the Spirit will not fail them. All the more that the Spirit who "hovered over" the Council did it for the sake of the people. He is *adest*, present, to them—intent to bring to good conclusion the work that he initiated, sustained, and completed through the ministry of his good servant Pope John and his Council.

But how could the people ever be "in session"—purposefully conversing on the ways and means of appropriating the Council's insights and responding to the Spirit, to the Spirit who wants them to be partners in re-creating the face of the church so that it be more and more, as Christ is, light to the nations? Is there any practical way "no less salutary than festive" or efficacious and merry (to quote Sir Thomas More) to lead the people increasingly into the intelligence of the Council's work and subsequent conversion?

Let this proposal be respectfully submitted:

Whereas the years from 2012 through 2015 will be the fiftieth anniversaries of the Council, they should be solemnly declared *the years of the Council*—when the entire people, "from the bishops to the last of the faithful" (LG 12, quoting St. Augustine), recalls the memory of the "Sacred Council" (SC 1), studies its determinations, and exposes itself to the transforming light and force of the Spirit—as the Council Fathers did. Over four years again, let the cry *Adsumus*, "we are present and attentive," resound—not within the walls of St. Peter's Basilica but throughout the face of the earth.

The Spirit of God will not fail to respond.

References

I wish to thank the following authors, editors, and publishers who graciously granted permission to reprint previously published material:

Chapter 1, "In Praise of *Communio,*" is a revised text of a presentation delivered at the meeting of the Canadian Canon Law Society on October 23, 2003, in London, Ontario, and published in *Studia Canonica* 38 (2004) 5–36.

Chapter 2, "Episcopal Conferences," is a revised version of the article "Die Bischofskonferenzen und die Macht des Geistes," published in *Stimmen der Zeit* 218 (2000) 3–18.

Chapter 4, "Toward the One Church of Christ," is a revised version of "A Time to Ponder: A Reflection on the Spiritual Mystery of the Ecumenical Movement," published in *America* (February 5, 2007); also in *Moral Theology for the Twenty-First Century*, edited by Bernard Hoose et al. (London: T & T Clark, 2008).

Chapter 5, "Reception of Laws," is a revised and enlarged version of a public lecture given at the Pontifical Oriental Institute in Rome, May 26, 1994, and of the article "The Reception of the Laws by the People of God," published in *The Jurist* 55 (1995) 504–26.

Chapter 6, "Law for Life," is a revised text of a talk given at the annual meeting of the Canon Law Society of America, October 3, 2005, at Tampa, Florida, and published in *The Jurist* 67 (2007) 15–18.

Chapter 7, "Justice in the Church," is a slightly revised text of "Gerechtigkeit in der Kirche," published in *Stimmen der Zeit* 216 (1998) 363–74.

Chapter 8, "Stability and Development in Canon Law," is a revised edition of "Stability and Development in Canon Law and the Case of 'Definitive' Teaching," published in *Notre Dame Law Review* 76 (2001) 865–79.

Chapter 9, "Definitive Doctrine and Ordinances Supporting It" contains an exchange previously published in German: Ladislas Orsy, "Von der Autorität kirchlicher Dokumente," in *Stimmen der Zeit* 216 (1998) 735–40; Joseph

Cardinal Ratzinger, "Stellungnahme," in *Stimmen der Zeit* 217 (1999) 169–72; Ladislas Orsy, "Antwort an Kardinal Ratzinger," in *Stimmen der Zeit* 217 (1999) 305–16; Joseph Cardinal Ratzinger, "Schlusswort zur Debatte mit Pater Orsy," in *Stimmen der Zeit* 217 (1999) 420–22.

Chapter 10, "In the Service of the Holy Spirit," is a revised version of a lecture given at the University of Leuven, Monsignor W. Onclin Chair 1998, and published in *Bridging Past and Future* (Leuven: Peeters, 1998) 33–53.

Bibliography

Standard encyclopedias, lexica, and commonly used reference works in theology and canon law are not listed.

Special References

Unless otherwise noted, except for occasional minor corrections to bring the English closer to the Latin text, all quotations from the Code of Canon Law are taken from the translation of the Canon Law Society of America: *Code of Canon Law: Latin-English Edition. New English Translation* (Washington, DC: Canon Law Society of America, 1999).

Scripture quotations are from the Revised Standard Version of the Bible, copyright 1952 [2nd edition, 1971] by the Division of Christian Education of the National Council of the Churches of Christ in the United States of America. Used by permission. All rights reserved.

Quotations in English from the documents of Vatican Council II are taken from *Vatican Council II: A Completely Revised Translation* (Dublin: Dominican Publications, 1996).

Books

The following list is a representative selection of books in which I found indispensible information, significant insights, promptings for counter insights, and questions worthy of debates. By citing them, I wish to acknowledge my indebtedness to their authors.

Alberigo, Giuseppe, ed. *L'Officina Bolognese, 1953–2003.* Bologna: EDB, 2004.

Alberigo, Giuseppe, and Joseph A. Komonchak, eds. *History of Vatican II.* 5 vols. Maryknoll, NY: Orbis, 1995, 1997, 2000, 2002, 2006.

Bobrinskoy, Boris. *Le mystère de l'Église: Cours de théologie dogmatique.* Paris: Cerf, 2003.

Boeglin, Jean-Georges. *La question de la Tradition dans la théologie catholique contemporaine.* Paris: Cerf, 1998.

Boeglin, Jean-Georges. *Pierre dans la communion des Églises: Le ministère pétrinien dans la perspective de l'Église-Communion et de la communion des Églises.* Paris: Cerf, 2004.

Bonnet, Piero Antonio, and Carlo Gullo, eds. *La Curia Romana nella Cost. Ap. "Pastor Bonus."* Vatican City: Libreria Editrice Vaticana, 1990.

Boudignon, Patrice. *Pierre Teilhard de Chardin: Sa vie, son œuvre, sa réflexion.* Paris: Cerf, 2008.

Bouyer, Louis. *The Decomposition of Catholicism.* Translated from the French. Eugene, OR: Wipf and Stock, 2002.

Braaten, Carl, and Robert Jenson, eds. *Church Unity and the Papal Office: An Ecumenical Dialogue on John Paul II's Encyclical "Ut unum sint."* Grand Rapids, MI: Eerdmans, 2001.

Burkhard, John J. *Apostolicity Then and Now: An Ecumenical Church in a Postmodern World.* Collegeville, MN: Liturgical Press, 2004.

Carter, Alex. *A Canadian Bishop's Memoirs.* North Bay, ON: Tomiko Publications, 1994.

Catherine of Siena. *The Dialogue.* Translated from the Italian. New York: Paulist Press, 1980.

Celeghin, Adriano. *Origine e natura della potestà sacra: Posizioni postconciliari.* Brescia: Morcelliana, 1987.

Chiron, Yves. *Frère Roger: Le Fondateur de Taizé.* Paris: Perin, 2008.

Clément, Olivier. *You are Peter: An Orthodox Theologian's Reflection on the Exercise of Papal Primacy.* New York: New City Press, 2003.

Clifford, Catherine. *The Groupe Des Dombes: A Dialogue of Conversion.* New York: Peter Lang, 2005.

Collins, Paul. *Papal Power: A Proposal for Change in Catholicism's Third Millennium.* London: HarperCollins, 1997.

Congar, Yves. *After Nine Hundred Years: The Background of the Schism Between the Eastern and Western Churches.* Translated from the French. New York: Fordham University, 1959.

Congar, Yves. *Droit ancien et structures ecclésiales.* London: Variorum Reprints, 1982.

Congar, Yves. *Écrits Réformateurs.* Paris: Cerf, 1995.

Congar, Yves. *Jalons pour une théologie du laïcat.* Revised edition, with addenda. Paris: Cerf, 1964.

Congar, Yves. *Journal d'un théologien, 1946–1956.* Paris: Cerf, 2000.

Congar, Yves. *La collégialité épiscopale: Histoire et théologie.* Paris: Cerf, 1965.

Congar, Yves. *L'Église: De saint Augustin à l'époque moderne.* Paris: Cerf, 1997.

Congar, Yves. *Ministères et communion ecclésiale: théologie sans frontières.* Paris: Cerf, 1971.

Congar, Yves. *Mon Journal du Concile.* 2 vols. Paris: Cerf, 2002.

Congar, Yves. *Vraie et fausse réforme dans l'Eglise.* Second revised and corrected edition. Paris: Cerf, 1968.

Congar, Yves, and B.D. Dupuy. *L'épiscopat et l'Église universelle.* Paris: Cerf, 1962.

Congregatio pro Doctrina Fidei. *Documenta inde a Concilio Vaticano Secundo expleto edita (1966–2005).* Vatican City: Libreria Editrice Vaticana, 2006.

Cozzens, Donald. *Sacred Silence: Denial and the Crisis in the Church.* Collegeville, MN: Liturgical Press, 2002.

de Lubac, Henri. *The Sources of Revelation.* Translated from the French. New York: Herder and Herder, 1968.

Dulles, Avery. *Models of the Church.* New York: Doubleday, 1991.

Dulles, Avery. *Church and Society.* New York: Fordham University, 2008.

Dupré, Louis. *Religion and the Rise of Modern Culture.* Notre Dame: University of Notre Dame, 2008.

Dupuis, Jacques. *Toward a Christian Theology of Religious Pluralism.* Maryknoll, NY: Orbis, 1997.

Erickson, John. *The Challenges of our Past: Studies in Orthodox Canon Law and Church History.* Crestwood, NY: St. Vladimir's Seminary, 1991.

Evans, Gillian R. *Method in Ecumenical Theology.* New York: Cambridge University, 1996.

Faggioli, Massimo. *Il Vescovo e il Concilio: Modello episcopale e aggiornamento al Vaticano II.* Bologna: Mulino, 2005.

Faivre, Alexandre. *Les laïcs aux origines de l'Église.* Paris: Centurion, 1979.

Faivre, Alexandre. *Naissance d'une hiérarchie: Les premières étapes du cursus clérical.* Paris: Béauchesne, 1977.

Fransen, Piet F. *Hermeneutics of the Councils and Other Studies.* Edited by H.E. Mertens and F. De Graeve. Leuven: Leuven University Press, 1985.

Gallagher, Clarence. *Church Law and Church Order in Rome and Byzantium: A Comparative Study.* Burlington, VT: Ashgate, 2002.

Gaudemet, Jean. *Église et cité: Histoire du droit canonique.* Paris: Montchrestien, 1994.

Geffré, Claude, and Gwendoline Jarczyk. *Profession théologien: Quelle pensée chrétienne pour le XXIe siècle?* Paris: Albin Michel, 1999.

Grootaers, Jan. *Le chantier reste ouvert: les laïcs dans l'Église et dans le monde.* Paris: Centurion, 1988.

Groupe des Dombes. *Pour la conversion des Églises: Identité et changement dans la dynamique de communion.* Paris: Centurion, 1991.

Haag, Herbert. *Nur wer sich ändert, bleibt sich treu: Für eine Verfassung der katholischen Kirche.* Freiburg in Br.: Herder, 2000.

Haight, Roger. *Dynamics of Theology.* Second edition. Maryknoll, NY: Orbis, 2001.

Hogan, Linda. *Confronting the Truth: Conscience in the Catholic Tradition.* London: Darton, Longman, and Todd, 2000.

Hoose, Bernard, Julie Clague, and Gerard Mannion, eds. *Moral Theology for the Twenty-First Century: Essays in Celebration of Kevin Kelly.* London: T and T Clark, 2008.

Huber, Christian. *Papst Paul VI und das Kirchenrecht.* Essen: Ludgerus, 1999.

Ishay, Micheline R. *The History of Human Rights: From Ancient Times to the Modern Era.* Berkeley: University of California, 2008.

Krätzl, Helmut. *Im Sprung gehemmt: Was wir nach dem Konzil noch alles fehlt.* Mödling: St. Gabriel, 1999.

Küng, Hans. *My Struggle for Freedom: Memoirs.* Translated from the German. Grand Rapids, MI: Eerdmans, 2003.

Lafont, Ghislain. *Imagining the Catholic Church: Structured Communion in the Spirit.* Translated from the French. Collegeville, MN: Liturgical Press, 2000.

Mahoney, Jack. *The Challenge of Human Rights: Origin, Development, and Science.* Oxford: Blackwell, 2007.

Marchetto, Agostino, ed. *Il Concilio Ecumenico Vaticano II: Contrappunto per la sua storia.* Vatican City: Libreria Editrice Vaticana, 2005.

McBrien, Richard. *The Church: The Evolution of Catholicism.* New York: HarperOne, 2008.

McDonagh, Enda. *Vulnerable to the Holy in Faith, Morality, and Art.* Blackrock, Co. Dublin: Columba Press, 2004.

McKenna, Kevin E. *The Battle for Rights in the United States Catholic Church.* Mahwah, NJ: Paulist Press, 2007.

Mühlen, Heribert. *Una Mystica Persona. Die Kirche als das Mysterium der heilsgeschichtlichen Identität des Heiligen Geistes in Christus und den Christen: Eine Person in vielen Personen.* Second edition. Munich: Schöningh, 1960.

Murray, Paul, ed. *Receptive Ecumenism and the Call to Catholic Learning: Exploring a Way for Contemporary Ecumenism.* Oxford: Oxford University, 2008.

Mußner, Franz. *Petrus und Paulus: Pole der Eineit.* Freiburg: Herder, 1976.

Naud, André. *Pour une éthique de la parole épiscopale.* Montréal: Fides, 2002.

Naud, André. *Un aggiornamento et son éclipse: La liberté de la pensée dans la foi et dans l'Église à Vatican II et aujourd'hui.* Québec: Fides, 1996.

Newman, John Henry. *An Essay on the Development of Christian Doctrine.* Notre Dame, IN: Notre Dame University, 1989.

Newman, John Henry. *On Consulting the Faithful in Matters of Doctrine.* Kansas City, MO: Sheed and Ward, 1961.

Noonan, John. *A Church That Can and Cannot Change: The Development of Catholic Moral Teaching.* Notre Dame, IN: University of Notre Dame, 2005.

O'Malley, John. *What Happened at Vatican II.* Cambridge, MA: Belknap, 2008.

Pottmeyer, Hermann J. *Towards a Papacy in Communion: Perspectives from Vatican Councils I & II.* Translated from the German. New York: Crossroad, 1998.

Pree, Helmuth. *Die evolutive Interpretation der Rechtsnorm im Kanonischen Recht.* Wien: Springer, 1980.

Puglisi, James, ed. *Petrine Ministry and the Unity of the Church: Toward a Patient and Fraternal Dialogue.* Collegeville, MN: Liturgical Press, 1997.

Rahner, Karl. *The Dynamic Element in the Church.* Translated from the German. New York: Herder and Herder, 1964.

Rahner, Karl, and Joseph Ratzinger. *The Episcopate and the Primacy.* Translated from the German. New York: Herder and Herder, 1962.

Reese, Thomas J., ed. *Episcopal Conferences: Historical, Canonical, and Theological Studies.* Washington, DC: Georgetown University, 1989.

Richter, von Klemens, ed. *Das Konzil war Erst der Anfang: Die Bedeutung des II. Vatikanums für Theologie und Kirche.* Mainz: Matthias-Grünewald, 1991.

Rigal, Jean. *L'église en quête d'avenir: Réflections et propositions pour des temps nouveaux.* Paris: Cerf, 2003.

Rigal, Jean. *Le mystère de l'Église: Fondements théologiques et perspectives pastorales.* Paris: Cerf, 1996.

Schatz, Klaus. *Papal Primacy: From Its Origins to the Present.* Translated from the German. Collegeville, MN: Liturgical Press, 1996.

Taylor, Charles. *A Secular Age.* Cambridge, MA: Belknap, 2007.

Thils, Gustave. *Les laïcs dans le nouveau Code de droit canonique et au IIe Concile du Vatican.* Louvain-la-Neuve: Faculté de Théologie, 1983.

Tihon, Paul, ed. *Changer la papauté?* Paris: Cerf, 2000.

Tillard, Jean Marie R. *Église d'églises: L'ecclésiologie de communion.* Paris: Cerf, 1987.

Tillard, Jean Marie R. *L'évêque de Rome.* Paris: Cerf, 1982.

Villemin, Laurent. *Pouvoir d'ordre et pouvoir de juridiction: Histoire théologique de leur distinction.* Paris: Cerf, 2003.

Voderholzer, Rudolf, and Michael J. Miller. *Meet Henri de Lubac.* San Francisco: Ignatius Press, 2007.

von Balthasar, Hans Urs. *Theodrama: Theological Dramatic Theory.* 2 vols. San Francisco: Ignatius Press, 1988, 1990.

Vorgrimler, Herbert, ed. *Commentary on the Documents of Vatican II.* 4 vols. Translated from the German. Second edition. New York: Herder and Herder, 1967.

Wackenheim, Charles. *Une Église au peril de ses lois.* Montréal: Novalis, 2007.

Index of Persons